THE ALPINE SET
IN SWITZERLAND

CHARLIE CHAPLIN, GRAHAM GREENE, FREDDIE MERCURY AND OTHER FAMOUS RESIDENTS

By the same author:

Fame and Fortune in Switzerland:
Audrey Hepburn, Richard Burton, Yul Brynner
and other celebrity residents

The Alpine Set in Switzerland

Charlie Chaplin, Graham Greene, Freddie Mercury and other famous residents

by

Lindsay Greatwood

John James Publications

List of Illustrations

Cover: *Alpine landscape* © 2010 Lindsay Stuby-Greatwood

Contents

Foreword

Darling, we're known as The Alpine Set! wrote the actress Benita Hume to a Hollywood friend in the late Sixties. She had just moved to the picturesque tax haven of Lausanne on Lake Geneva with her husband, matinée idol George Sanders. George had many reasons for wanting to enjoy the clean air and mountain views of Switzerland: he could keep most of the money he earned from various and unusual sources and enjoy the highest standard of living; he was only an hour by air from the major European movie capitals and he would avoid being hounded by Hollywood gossip columnists who wanted to know more about his past and present. Most of all, he could continue to build a financial scam that stretched from Italy to Los Angeles and would take in the British government and a good number of famous Swiss residents.

If you want peace, come to Switzerland, the rock singer and Montreux resident Freddie Mercury was to tell the world a decade or so after George Sanders was obliged to leave the country. Peace was certainly what Belgian thriller writer Georges Simenon sought when he moved to Lausanne from the United States at the end of the 1950's. Peace from the tax man and a chance to repair his ailing marriage. He would build a magnificent ranch-style house on a hillside above Lake Geneva where his neighbour Charlie Chaplin would visit him and discuss matters that concern the rich and famous, such as how to deal with those who wished to relieve them of their wealth. When the two men compared begging letters they'd received, they were amused to find they were getting requests for money from the same individual.

It could have been the kidnapping of Charlie Chaplin's body, not long after the world-famous comedian had been laid to rest, that influenced Simenon's decision to be cremated. Charlie's wife, Oona, was not amused when her husband's grave was dug over, one rainy night, and his body taken away and held to ransom. There would follow a chase along the Swiss Riviera, worthy of Chaplin's early cop one-reelers. But the Swiss police already had a good deal of practice in chasing fraudsters around Lake Geneva and would work closely with other organisations, such as Interpol and the FBI, to put an end to an international business scam that would stretch all the way to the north of Scotland.

The writer Graham Greene was sure he'd found a brilliant lawyer in Lausanne who would take care of the fortune his books and films were generating. The lawyer was a business associate of the actor George Sanders. Greene would be a lot poorer as a result of the lawyer's arrest, but not as poor as Sanders, who would be found dead in a hotel room, not many years afterwards. Another writer who had a narrow financial escape when Sanders and his associates had their activities curtailed was the thriller writer James Hadley Chase who lived in the wine-growing village of Corseaux, not far from the comedian Charlie Chaplin and their friend, actor James Mason.

Mason arrived in Corseaux after an expensive Hollywood divorce, sat on a tea chest in a bare room and tried to sort out his life. He had already received a phone call from his friend George Sanders when he'd first arrived in Hollywood, with a suggestion for a sure-fire way of making money. But James's first-class acting ability and his distinctive voice would enable him to build a comfortable life in Switzerland's low-taxed land where, unlike his old friend George, he would keep hold of his wealth. Mason would also get to know Vladimir Nabokov, the writer of one of his best known films, the classic tale of *Lolita*. Mason and the Russian author would be near-neighbours in the 1960's and 1970's, often dining together at the luxury hotel Les Trois Couronnes where Henry James had set part of his novel, *Daisy Miller*.

Switzerland was an ideal bolt-hole for international writers such as Georges Simenon, Graham Greene, James Hadley Chase, A. J. Cronin, author of the Doctor Finlay books, Eric Ambler, the Hollywood screenwriter who wrote *The Mask of Dimitrios*, and Edgar Wallace, author of *The Four Just Men* and *The Forger*. Edgar Wallace would spend holidays in Caux, in the heights above Montreux, while Ernest Hemingway would gain inspiration for *A Farewell to Arms* from his stay in the village of Chamby, nearby. Noël Coward, a close friend of several famous Swiss residents profiled in *Fame and Fortune in Switzerland*, such as Richard Burton, Peter Ustinov, Audrey Hepburn and Yul Brynner, spent many happy years in the village of Les Avants near Montreux and would take the local train across the mountains to visit his friend, actor David Niven, at Château-d'Oex.

Montreux, with its micro-climate and palm trees, was where Vladimir Nabokov would make his home, in the grand Montreux Palace Hotel overlooking the lake. Nabokov, whose family had owned large estates in Russia before the 1917 Revolution, had changed country several times before finally settling in Switzerland. He occupied the hotel suite below that of actor Peter Ustinov, whose parents had also been forced to flee Russia. Both men saw their stay at the hotel as a temporary one, but only Ustinov and his family moved on. When he did so, Nabokov and his wife, Véra, took over Peter's suite at the top of the hotel, with its breathtaking views of the Dents du Midi mountains. After years of rented accommodation, in Hitler's Germany, in Vichy France and on several university campuses in America, the Nabokovs had lost the habit of living in domestic surroundings. Nabokov would often work in the early hours of the morning, when the hotel was quiet and its guests abed. But the age of rock stars would soon bring a different sort of hotel clientèle.

When singer Freddie Mercury first stayed at the Montreux Palace Hotel, he was exuberant enough to swing from one of the hotel chandeliers. As the years went by and he returned to Montreux to record his albums, he grew to love the mountain air and the lakeside views. He would eventually buy his own home on the waterfront and record his last songs with his group, Queen, in their Mountain Studios. Freddie enjoyed a privacy in Switzerland that was impossible in London, particularly in the last years of his life. After his death, a commemorative statue of the singer was erected by the lake, close to his recording studio and Swiss home. It stands only metres from another bronze statue, that of Vladimir Nabokov, which also gazes across the water to the Alps beyond. Further along the road, in Vevey, stands another statue, that of Charlie Chaplin in his famous ill-fitting clothes and bowler hat with bent cane. He also looks out at the mountain view which brought him so much peace, after years of struggling against every kind of authority.

Always careful with money, Chaplin fought every tax demand the American Inland Revenue Service tossed at him. But it was the CIA, rather than the IRS, who finally drove him from American shores to Switzerland. Charlie, who had lived in poverty in his childhood, was an admirer of Communist economic theory and gave speeches in the States, asking people to help the Russian effort against Hitler during World War Two. When he addressed his audiences as 'comrades', the CIA pricked up its ears and opened a file on him. It was made clear to the comedian that if he left the country he would find it difficult to return. At the height of McCarthyism, Charlie took his family to Europe, never to live in America again.

Graham Greene wrote an open letter to Charlie in the *New Statesman*, defending the entertainer's beliefs and storing up trouble for himself. Like Chaplin, Greene had had his share of troubles with tax authorities and the CIA, but his journey to Switzerland had taken a very different path, in a life as dramatic and eventful as any of his novels.

A licence to print money was how Hollywood star George Sanders saw the investment scam he'd hatched with Thomas Roe, Lausanne lawyer and friend of many wealthy individuals, such as Graham Greene. James Mason was fortunate that, by the time he joined his fellow-actor, Sanders, in Switzerland, he had little money to spare for George's grandiose schemes. He was able to rebuild his life and his finances in Switzerland but, because of a family dispute, his ashes remained in a bank vault until his daughter finally located them, sixteen years after his death.

Like Charlie Chaplin, novelist Vladimir Nabokov left the United States in the 1950's to return to Europe. Like his fellow-writer, Georges Simenon, Nabokov missed the European way of life, although he knew he would never see his beloved Russia again. Unlike Chaplin, Nabokov was no admirer of Russian Communism, which he saw as a destroyer of landscapes and beautiful buildings, as well as the national spirit. The wooded slopes around Montreux reminded Nabokov of the countryside near St Petersburg where he had roamed as a boy, catching butterflies, sketching and painting nature and writing poetry. The writer would buy a plot of land next to his friend Peter Ustinov in the mountain ski-resort of Les Diablerets, near Montreux, but, unlike Peter, he would never build a home there. He would roam the alpine slopes with his butterfly net, pursuing his lifetime's interest in lepidoptery, even into his seventies. Once, at Davos, the writer slithered down a slope and lost hold of his net which lodged in a nearby fir tree. Trying to reach it, Nabokov fell again and was unable to stand upright. When a cable car passed above him, he frantically waved for help. The passengers looked down at the old man and smiled and waved back. When the cable car made its return journey, the operator saw Nabokov, still lying in the same place, and called out the emergency services. Two and a half hours after his fall, Vladimir Nabokov was taken off the mountainside, but he quickly recovered and went back to chasing butterflies on the mountain slopes.

It's possible that the mountain scenery around Lake Geneva reminded rock star Freddie Mercury, like Nabokov, of his carefree schooldays in another land. Freddie Bulsara, as Mercury was known at boarding school, had left the East African spice island of Zanzibar, where he was born, to receive a thoroughly British education in the verdant hills of Panchgani, near Bombay in India, home of his relatives. With British super-tax at 83% of Freddie's income, he and his group, Queen, were happy to work in recording studios abroad. The group bought Mountain Studios in the casino complex on the Montreux waterfront, where other names in rock, such as David Bowie, Status Quo, Iggy Pop and The Rolling Stones would also record their hits. Queen's album *Jazz* was named after the Montreux Jazz Festival, which was in full swing when the group came to town. It was during a Frank Zappa performance in the casino, one December, several years earlier, that a fan let off a firework and the hall caught fire. Mountain winds fed the flames and a pall of smoke hung over Lake Geneva. The group Deep Purple, who were in the audience, later composed the memorable song: *Smoke on the Water*, singing the praises of those who led the audience to safety that night.

Freddie Mercury composed his famous music hall pastiche *Killer Queen* with Montreux resident Noël Coward's style of melody and lyrics in mind. Like Freddie, Noël experienced setbacks before he became rich and famous and moved to Switzerland. There, he entertained many members of the Alpine Set, including Hollywood actor George Sanders. George, like Freddie Mercury, was a singer of songs and lover of life. But his life, like that of so many of Switzerland's Alpine Set, didn't work out exactly as planned.

Map of the Swiss Riviera

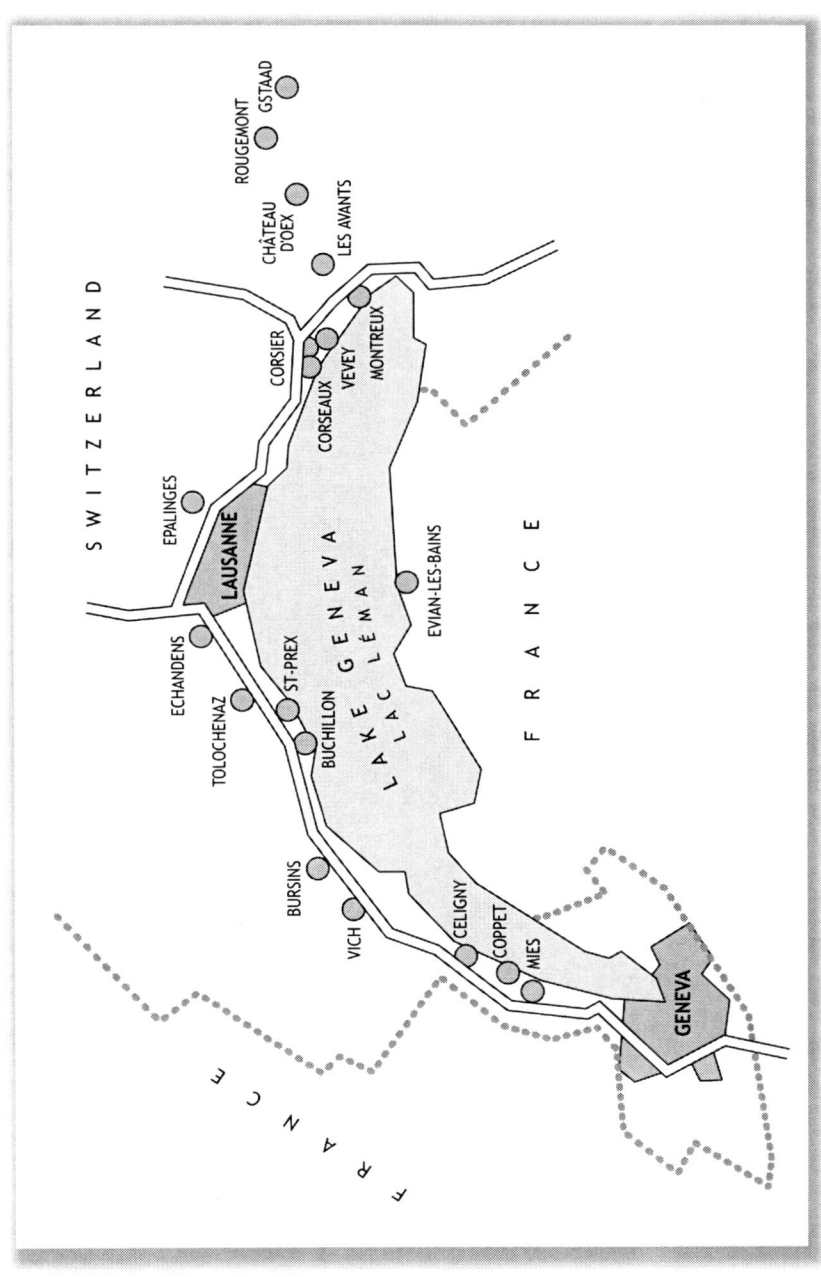

THE ALPINE SET IN SWITZERLAND

CHARLIE CHAPLIN, GRAHAM GREENE, FREDDIE MERCURY AND OTHER FAMOUS RESIDENTS

Chapter 1

Georges Simenon

Paris, 1935; a balmy September evening. The nightclub was an expensive one. The gypsy guitarist finished his solo and gave an almost imperceptible nod towards the table where Georges Simenon sat, regaling a group of diners with tales from his days as a cub reporter. Jean Cocteau glanced at Yul Brynner, levered himself up from the table, made his excuses to Georges and headed for the door. It was too early in the evening to abandon the best company in town: Simenon, the celebrated writer and raconteur, his artist wife and his erstwhile black mistress, and the lionised American novelist, Henry Miller, with his attractive bohemian lover, Anaïs Nin. But Cocteau fully intended to return to this sparkling group once he'd met with the Russian gypsy and got his fix. He saw the guitarist leave by the back. He went out through the foyer, refusing his coat from the hat check girl, past the doorman and into the street.

In a narrow alley behind the club, Brynner stood with his hands in his pockets, waiting. 'So, who are your glitzy pals?' he asked, watching the effete writer-artist count, limp-wristed, from a wad of notes under the lamplight.

Cocteau drew a quick breath and tutted. He was not in the mood for conversation. He needed the opium, now. The Russian musician could always be relied on to get the drug for him: he knew the sailors down at the docks. It wouldn't be right to upset the *immigré*; he depended on the young gypsy a lot. 'The man with the bow-tie is – '

'I know. I read the papers. He writes those detective stories. Seems to have a new one out every other month. Who's the blonde with him?'

Cocteau almost snatched the packet Brynner handed him, then relaxed a little, but he spoke fast. 'His wife, the artist they call Tigy. The coloured girl's – '

'Everyone knows Josephine Baker,' interrupted Yul, 'and her ass. Great mover. Best dancer in town.'

'She was his bit on the side, for a while. Wanted to marry him, Sim says. But he's always been good at telling stories.' Cocteau hurried his words, impatient to get away now. 'The other guy is a writer, too. His name's Henry Miller. Written some porn that won't get published in the

States. That's his girlfriend with him, Anaïs Nin, not the wife. She's helped to get his book published. Thanks for getting the stuff.' Cocteau started to walk away.

'Let me know when you want some more,' Brynner called out to Cocteau's receding back. The artist turned the corner and Yul was left, staring down an empty alleyway at grimy walls half-covered in fly posters and a couple of scrawny cats lurking by a lamp post. He examined the money in his hand, frowned for a moment, screwed the notes into a ball and jammed them in his pocket. 'One day,' he said out loud, addressing the cats that had looked up from their business. 'One day, I swear, I'll be rich and famous like that Simenon guy, and I'll have a beautiful wife and a sexy mistress, and I'll sit at the best tables in the most expensive clubs, and I won't be dealing shit in stinking alleyways any more.' The cats lost interest in him and rubbed around lamp post again. 'I'll work as hard as they say Georges Simenon works, and I'll play as hard as him, too. I'll have a swanky apartment and fast cars and good clothes. The man has it all. No wonder he laughs and drinks champagne while he enjoys his women. If I had the money he has, I'd be the happiest guy in the world, too. No troubles, the good life ... ' Brynner trailed back to the club, just in time to see Simenon give the doorman a fat tip and step into a taxi with his fur-coated ladies and his friends. Cocteau's head was just visible as the vehicle sped away. 'I swear, one day ... '

The night of February twelfth 1903 was icy cold in Liège, and raining. The city streets were deserted and most Belgian folk were slumbering as the clock hands edged towards midnight. But, in the commercial district of

Outremeuse, a slight, balding, solitary figure stood under a window, listening to the cries of his wife in childbirth. He dared not ascend the stairs. He took his watch from his waistcoat pocket for the fifth time in less than half an hour. One minute to midnight. Henriette had dreaded their first-born coming into the world on Friday the thirteenth, but it seemed there was no avoiding it.

Désiré closed the watch lid thoughtfully and looked up again at the lighted window. He had been standing there, in the drizzle, for five hours. How much longer could this go on, he wondered? Suddenly, he heard his wife give a long, agonised scream. Then, there was silence. He sprinted up the stone steps, flung open the front door and took the narrow stairs, two at a time. In the small room his exhausted wife lay, eyes half-closed and her head sunk in the big pillow. Beside her, the midwife had laid the new-born child, its face wrinkled and green with bronchitis. 'It's a boy, m'sieur,' he heard the woman say as she closed the door behind her, leaving the family alone together. Désiré glanced at his wife, who appeared to be sleeping, then quietly drew out his watch again and looked at the hands. 'Husband,' came Henriette's tired voice from the pillow, 'little Georges was born on the twelfth. Remember that when you go to the town hall and make the declaration for the birth certificate.' Her voice began to waver. 'I couldn't bear it if ... ' She started to sob.

'There, my love. Don't fret,' Désiré frowned and squeezed his wife's shoulder. 'No one's going to think or say bad things about us. He was born on the twelfth.' Henriette sank back into the pillow and closed her eyes again. The insurance clerk looked at his wife and shook his head. He had known when he'd married Henriette

Brüll that she lived in fear of being a social outsider. Appearances were everything to her. And no wonder; she had been traumatised by a series of cruel blows in her childhood. He looked at the wheezing baby and said a prayer for his newborn son. O Lord, may little Georges enjoy a tranquil, uneventful life and may he be content with a steady job at a modest but regular salary, just like mine.

Yet Désiré Simenon had a secret, something he dared not tell his wife. For Henriette, he knew, had ambitions for him and his job. Désiré earned 150 francs a month as a senior clerk at the local branch of Agences Générales et la Winterthur in Liège, in the fire insurance department, and he had recently turned down the chance to work the streets selling the new life insurance policies that were becoming popular. There had been a rare old scene when Henriette had found out Désiré had decided to stay put in his quiet, comfortable job at the office. What the clerk had not revealed to his wife was that he'd applied for life insurance cover himself and had been rejected when it was found that he had an enlarged heart.

Henriette's fear of financial insecurity was understandable, given her family background and her experiences in her formative years. Her father had been a prosperous dyke master, financed by his rich father-in-law, and the family had lived in an impressive farmhouse on the Zuid-Willemsvart Canal. Henriette was the last of her parents' thirteen children and, by the time she was born, her father was on a slippery financial slope downwards, assisted by his partiality to drink. A couple of bad business deals and her father's occupation was listed as a 'wholesale grocer', then 'domestic servant', then 'timber merchant'. When Henriette was only four, her father died, leaving her formerly wealthy mother to try to keep up appearances. Madame Brüll struggled to bring up the family while attempting to turn around her late husband's failing coal and timber company. The family were constantly on the move, from one address to another, and always living in poverty. In later years, Henriette would recall seeing her mother regularly place a pot of water on the range to steam away and give the impression to callers that she was just about to prepare a meal.

The girl grew up fearing poverty and spent the rest of her life fretting that disaster was just around the corner. With Désiré Simenon, she hoped to achieve financial security and social respectability, for she saw the two as interconnected. Needless to say, her two sons, Georges and his younger brother Christian, would absorb her daily anxieties, her need for order and stability, and be affected by them in their own adult lives.

But, due in part to his closeness to his more easy-going father, Georges Simenon did not inherit his mother's social inferiority complex. On the contrary, he was a bold teenager, almost to the point of rebelliousness; always testing authority and the patience of both his parents. Whereas his father would forgive, and even cover for the boy's boisterous behaviour, his mother simply transferred her affection to her more pliable and passive younger son, whom she considered 'a good boy'. Georges was never to forget his mother's obvious favouritism and, deeply wounded by what he saw as the unfairness of it all, would take his revenge in scathing descriptions of

Henriette and characterisations based on her in his novels and non-fiction in years to come.

Georges hero-worshipped his father and used his character as the heroic protagonist in many of his stories. His father's pipe-smoking became Georges's and Inspector Maigret's comforting habit. Maigret's dictum that one should 'understand and not judge,' was a characteristic Simenon saw in his father. Perhaps this is why Désiré uttered not a word when his wife filled the house with lodgers to boost their income, leaving her husband a cot-like space off the kitchen in which to sleep and read his newspaper. Georges spent more and more time in the local library and was a good student at school until he reached his teenage years. But it was, perhaps, the First World War and the social dislocation that wartime brought to Belgium which affected the eleven year-old boy the most. The horrors he saw and experienced in Liège during those years would remain with him and surface in his stories, time and again.

Like Audrey Hepburn, during the occupation of her country in the Second World War, young Simenon was to know hunger and fear in the years following 1914 as inhabitants of the town were shot for resisting the invaders. Like Audrey, he was forced to hide in the cellar with neighbours and roam the countryside for food. He saw corruption, by the invaders and the invaded, and saw his mother take in German soldiers, against his father's wishes, to replace the income she'd lost when her lodgers left at the outbreak of war. But the real horrors of war came home to the boy when he witnessed the excesses of the Armistice: the mob violence inflicted on those who were considered to have collaborated with the Germans during the years of occupation. He saw shop windows smashed and stock looted while the police looked on, helpless to control the crowds, and he saw the retribution meted out to women who were thought to have fraternised with the invaders, their hair cropped and their clothes torn from them, then forced to run through the streets.

Georges was fifteen when the war ended in 1918. He had started the Occupation as an altar boy and Grade-A student; he ended the war as a black marketeer who drank and womanised and was beyond parental control. There were physical fights with his mother while his father tried to keep the peace. When his father had a heart attack, Georges seized the moment to leave school and lead his own life. But a spell as a pastry chef in a local patisserie, followed by a short period working in a bookshop, made him realise that his lack of exam qualifications would keep him on the lower rungs of life unless he took action.

He had always loved writing at school and was particularly good at it. He had written essays for his fellow students, as well as his own, with ease and at great speed. The editor of the *Gazette de Liège* put him on probation and Simenon proved himself to be an ace reporter. It was the perfect job for him and the perfect experience for a future novelist. For the next four years, Georges was in his element: he had his own newspaper column and became a keen crime reporter. The editor was indulgent, paying him a good wage and allowing for his drinking, although his behaviour nearly got him the sack on one occasion.

As well as alcohol, Simenon had discovered the delights of women. He had lost his virginity at fifteen, as a schoolboy, and now he would often not bother to go home after work but go straight on to nightclubs with friends or enjoy the local prostitutes, or both. He was still able to knock out good copy for the paper and write short stories and publish a novel. His next two novels remained unpublished, but the first one had sold well. His artist friends had illustrated the book and, soon, Simenon was to write another, based on this crowd of bohemian pals.

They called themselves 'La Caque', which meant a barrel full of herrings so tightly packed that there was no room to move, and their sign was a scorpion biting its own tail. Their other symbol was even darker: a dead man hanging from the stone gargoyle of a church. They would meet and talk all night, fuelled by drink and other stimulants, and enjoy the women who joined them in a loft above a carpenter's shop. The meetings were wild, hedonistic affairs and it was only a matter of time before there were casualties. When one of their number was found hanged from a church door, Simenon, who had been with the young painter only hours before, was deeply affected by his death, the cause of which was never established. Georges was never questioned about the incident: how a comatose drug addict could have been capable of engineering his own suicide. An account of the death appeared, unsigned, in the *Gazette* the following morning and the incident was reworked in more than one of Simenon's novels.

On New Year's Eve, December 1920, Georges and some other members of 'La Caque' were out drinking, as usual, when a young gent asked them along to a party at his parents' home. The young man was an architect and he had a sister who was in her last year of studies at the Beaux-Arts academy. It is nothing short of miraculous that Régine Renchon, or Tigy as Simenon was soon to call her, took an interest in him that evening: the seventeen and a half year-old journalist was so drunk that he came in through her parents' front door on his hands and knees. But, as Simenon gradually sobered up, the talented art student, who had already successfully exhibited her work, talked to him about art and literature. Tigy was three years older than Georges and quite different from his usual diet of prostitutes. He adored her company and they soon became lovers and made plans for a future together. As a result, Simenon brought forward his military service so they could marry as soon as possible, then leave the city of Liège for the bright lights of Paris.

Not that the eighteen year-old, already an excellent journalist and a budding novelist, altered his lifestyle a great deal once he was engaged to be married. Later that year, on the 28 November 1921, he went to Antwerp on a story for his paper but spent much of the day in a hotel room with a distant female relative. As his train drew into the station that evening, he saw, to his surprise, Tigy and her father standing on the platform, waiting for him with serious faces. Jules Renchon gently broke the news to Georges that his adored father, Désiré, had collapsed in his office and died of a heart attack.

Simenon was stunned, and immediately felt guilty for all the trouble he'd caused his father during his rebellious teenage years. He also saw the futility of a supposedly 'safe' job: Désiré had died with only three hundred francs in his pocket. It was all the money the insurance clerk had in the world and it was not enough to pay for his funeral. Georges did the rounds of his more wealthy relatives, asking for help with the burial expenses.

Every one of the family refused to help and the young reporter was obliged to ask his employer at the newspaper for a loan. Once Désiré was laid to rest, one of his uncles removed the more valuable family furniture from the Simenons' home. Georges never forgot this and, decades later, when living a life of luxury in Switzerland, he made a point of writing about the treatment of his penniless, grieving family by his comfortable and uncaring relatives, all those years before.

The marriage of Georges and Tigy Simenon took place in Liège on 23 March 1923, and the bride wore black. George had already left for Paris three months earlier, after the death of his father, but, for the sake of his mother, Tigy the atheist agreed to a church wedding before they began their life together in France. Simenon had already found a job with a war veterans' publication there, but was frustrated by starting his career again at virtually messenger-boy status. He also missed his soul mate, Tigy, and wrote love letters to her, often tearfully, several times a day. He noted the rising popularity of the detective novel, along with that of the cinema, and told his fiancée he would do whatever was necessary to become a successful writer in Paris. Three months later, he returned to Liège for their wedding but, that very same evening, he and Tigy boarded the train for Paris to begin a new life in the artistic capital of the world.

Tigy produced paintings to help their finances while Georges continued with his dull day job and wrote short stories and pot boilers with amazing speed, out of office hours. These were the first signs of the phenomenal Simenon industry that would soon run to several novels a month and over four hundred fictional and non-fiction books by the time he died, as well as innumerable articles and short stories. After six months as a virtual office boy at the veterans' newspaper, 'Sim', as Georges was to be known for the next decade or so, was hired as a private secretary by the wealthy Marquis de Tracy. Simenon travelled around France, from château to château, with this rich aristocrat and the experience would bring him yet further material for his stories, particularly the Inspector Maigret novels.

But it was his short stories that were already finding a market and Georges was particularly keen on becoming a regular contributor to the national newspaper, *Le Matin*. He sent some of his work to the paper's literary editor, Colette, the famous author of *Chéri*, who would later discover Audrey Hepburn for the film version of her novel, entitled *Gigi*. Colette wrote back to Simenon, criticising the writer's stiff style. Don't be so 'literary'! she told him, and he realised he had to simplify and hone his writing, using fewer words and making every one of them count.

Once Georges had his new story-telling technique in place, he was on his way. He became a full-time writer with hours of free time to wander around Paris, since he produced work at an incredible speed. He was also an astute businessman, never writing for an advance, which he felt could lead to a false sense of wealth, and negotiating higher royalties instead. He also realised that short novels paid better than short stories and was soon producing pulp fiction under several different names. Within five years of living in Paris, Simenon was a successful and sought after writer with a knack for self-promotion. He never had an agent and he worked for several publishers and publications at the same time. The couple's income and lifestyle improved markedly and not only were they able to buy a car but hire a chauffeur, as well.

In 1925, Tigy and George took their first holiday. A friend lent them his house in Normandy and while they were there they hired a local fisherman's daughter, eighteen year-old Henriette Liberge, as a maid for Tigy. Georges soon christened the girl Boule and she became a permanent fixture in the Simenon household. She was also, unbeknown to Tigy, Georges's live-in mistress for many years. Fidelity was never Simenon's strong point but his marriage seemed to work, even when he conducted a passionate affair with the celebrated American Negro singer and dancer, Josephine Baker.

Josephine exuded sensuality; her body was made for love. Simenon found their coupling an earth-moving experience. For a while, in 1927, the cabaret star's energetic passion drained him and his writing output declined considerably. But Georges was too ambitious to lose a grip on his career and he decided to take a break from Paris and its diversions and temptations. A summer holiday near La Rochelle was all that it took. When the Simenons returned to the capital in the autumn, 'Sim' was back in his productive mode.

Paris continued to provide Georges with material for his stories but he was searching for a new vehicle for his ideas. He wanted to write less 'romantic' fiction and more about the criminal world. The following spring, the Simenons and Boule, plus their Great Dane, took a six month canal boat trip around France. As usual, the writer absorbed everything he came across: sounds, sights and smells. 1928 would see his output rise to forty-four novels published that year.

Boat trips worked for Simenon, and the next one would keep him away from Paris for three years. It would also produce his most famous character, a police inspector who would be known and read all over the globe. The Simenons, plus Boule and dog, set off from Paris in their custom-built fishing cutter, the *Ostrogoth*, in the spring of 1929, heading north for the flat lands of Holland and Belgium, far from the distractions of *la belle France* and their good-time friends in Paris. Simenon felt he was close to something new in his writing; a character called Inspector Maigret had begun to appear in his novels. Holland inspired the first real Maigret story, *Pietr-le-Letton*, though Simenon was later to give several versions of how he came to visualise the bowler-hatted, pipe-smoking sleuth. By 1930, he had found a new direction and began to write under his own name, instead of the many pseudonyms he'd been using since he'd come to Paris. In February 1931, the writer organised a grand fancy dress ball on the theme of police and criminals to publicise his Maigret series. The evening was a great success and the novels that followed made Simenon's fortune. Based in part on the character of the author himself, Simenon found he could write a 'Maigret' in a matter of days. But writing at speed was exhausting and, soon, Georges was ready for yet another change of scenery; this time on the west coast of France.

In 1932, the Simenons took a lease on a house in La Rochelle and, leaving Boule to run the place, they took off for Africa where Georges used the experience to produce articles and novels. His *romans durs*, the darker psychological novels, began to appear in 1933 and, in 1934, the Simenons sailed the Mediterranean for the summer before taking the lease on a château in the forest of Orléans. But Georges felt less dependent on Tigy than he had done at the beginning of their marriage, and setting off for a world tour with her, for eight months in 1935, helped neither his marriage nor his book productivity.

The couple returned to Paris and bought a luxury apartment opposite the Bois de Boulogne. Tigy busied herself with expensive decorations while Georges got back to work, producing a couple of novels before the end of the year. But he was not happy with his grand lifestyle and, although he embraced Paris nightlife once more, frequenting Fouquet's and Maxim's and enjoying the company of Picasso, Cocteau, Rothschild and other luminaries, he could see his social life was affecting his work. It was during this period that the young Yul Brynner began to earn his living as a guitarist in the capital's night clubs - and supplying Simenon's friend, Cocteau, with his favourite recreational drug.

But Georges, like many others, saw the good times were about to end. War with Germany was now a distinct possibility, and Simenon knew, from his childhood experiences in World War One, what effect a situation like that could have on a society. He also knew that cities were not the place to be, with bombs raining down and insufficient food for the inhabitants. In 1938 he returned to the west coast, bought a house by the sea and, after fourteen years of restless wanderings, Tigy decided it was the right moment to become pregnant.

Simenon had already joined a pacifist movement in Paris but was ready, as a reservist, to serve his mother country. He headed for Belgium, but the Munich Agreement delayed mobilisation and he returned thankfully to La Rochelle and his books. He was beginning to be known as a serious writer, earning praise from authors such as André Gide and François Mauriac. He even believed he would win the Nobel Prize for literature. He immersed himself in his characters, their situations and their personalities, bringing them to life on the page. He was also consuming a certain amount of red wine each day, such was the stress he put himself under during the composition of a novel.

Marc Simenon was born on 19 April 1939 in Belgium. Georges, his famous imagination working overtime, had been terrified that his child would be born with some kind of defect and he had rushed Tigy, now in her eighth month of pregnancy, across France to the best doctors he knew. They went, first of all, to Strasbourg, then on to Brussels, where the writer was so nervous as his wife gave birth that he rushed from the hospital and threw up.

The family returned to the countryside near La Rochelle and Simenon prepared to sit out the war as uneventfully as possible. His writing was going well, his son was adorable, his wife was fulfilled and their maid, Boule, ran their home for them. But, when Belgium was invaded, he knew where his duty lay and, with a heavy heart, he dressed in his own version of a Belgian reservist's uniform and left for his country's embassy in Paris to volunteer his services. To his relief, he was ordered back to La Rochelle to oversee the reception of thousands of Belgian refugees as they poured into the area.

Organisation was one of Georges Simenon's strengths. Over the years, it had helped him produce articles and novels at speed and in quantity. Now, he threw himself into his new role as Commissioner for Belgian Refugees, well aware that he had been spared the danger of combat duties. With other officials, he set up a camp and reception centre and, as the fighting intensified and the number of displaced persons multiplied, he and his neighbours fed and housed the refugees in their own homes. Georges would ferry the homeless about, cramming up to twelve people at a time in his canary yellow convertible. But the coast was under continual bombardment, first by the Germans, then by the British. The Simenons' house narrowly escaped being engulfed by flames when the petrol refinery next door was hit. When France surrendered in June 1939, Georges's commission came to an end and, when a German officer was quartered in the Simenons' house, it was time for the family to look for another home in the region.

They rented a farmhouse for a few weeks, then spent a couple of years living in the wing of a château. In 1942, they headed north to a remote hamlet in the Vendée where Georges got down to some serious gardening, producing food for their table and for barter, and gathering fuel for their fire. These were mainly idyllic times for the family, although Georges and Tigy were considered aliens and had to report to the local police station at first. Simenon was able to continue his work and even take trips to Paris. There was a bad moment when he was accused of being Jewish, which he wasn't, and of being a black marketeer, which he almost certainly was. Simenon felt threatened enough to write an article which was not wholly complimentary to Jewish businessmen, then hunkered down and got on with his writing.

Liberation would bring other complications, but the last major disruption in the Simenon household before the end of the war was to be a domestic one. One afternoon, in April 1944, Tigy discovered her husband in bed with Boule, their housekeeper. Tigy demanded that Boule be dismissed but Georges would not hear of it, pointing out that, if they were arrested as aliens, Boule would be there for young Marc. And, anyway, explained Georges, he had been unfaithful to Tigy with plenty of other women. Tigy talked of divorce, but neither of them wanted to be without Marc. They agreed to continue the marriage as friends, for the child's sake, and give each other their freedoms.

Georges had managed to keep his output and income buoyant during the war years and several of his books were adapted for the cinema by the Nazi-controlled French film company, Continental. The writer knew, from what he'd witnessed in Liège in 1918, that liberation was the moment when old scores and jealousies were settled in the name of *épuration*: the purging of those who'd fraternised or collaborated with the enemy. By the summer of 1944, undisciplined bands in the French Resistance, the FFI, were meting out their own form of justice to those they felt deserved it. It was one quiet and sunny afternoon, when Simenon was tending his vegetable garden, that a group claiming to be from the FFI came to call.

Boule had answered the door to them. The writer was out, she told them. They said they'd return in an hour. Boule nodded, smiled and waved as she unhurriedly closed the front door. Then she flew down the back path to the vegetable patch and told Georges what had happened. The moment was not totally unexpected and the writer was quick to react. He slipped behind a tall hedge while Boule ran and fetched the rucksack his wife had packed for such an event. A trusted neighbour was contacted and, with food, clothes and medicine, Georges was hidden in a nearby barn until Tigy, Marc and Boule were able to join him. They camped out with some others, including the village doctor, in a little-known field where they could remain hidden.

By the time the family were able to return home, the over-imaginative Simenon was suffering from nervous exhaustion and pleurisy. They moved house again, in an effort to distance themselves from Paris as the liberated mob took to the streets. Some of Georges's friends, including the actor Michel Simon who had done nothing worse than tour Germany during the war with a delegation of French artistes, were not so lucky and several were forced into hiding. Coco Chanel was arrested and fled to Switzerland. Simenon knew he would also have to leave France and plans were set in motion.

It was while Georges was arranging visas for a supposed working trip to the United States that he received a message that a man seated on a bench in the gardens of his apartment building needed to see him urgently. It was his younger brother, Christian, who had spent part of the war in the Belgian Rexist movement, a Fascist organisation that had carried out attacks on resistance fighters. He had been one of their drivers and was now running for his life. He needed help and he needed money. Georges was able to give him both.

The writer suggested his brother join the French Foreign Legion under an assumed name until life calmed down at home. The Legion didn't ask questions and a number of collaborators were able to disappear in this way. Unfortunately, Christian was killed on active service in Vietnam in 1947 when his unit was attacked by the Viet-Minh. He left a fifteen year-old son he hadn't seen since the war and Simenon was racked with guilt, since it had been his suggestion that his brother join up. Georges looked after his nephew, as he'd promised he would, should anything happen to Christian, but his mother, back in Liège, could only lament, 'Why did it have to be him instead of you? You killed him!'

Tigy and Georges left France for the United States, via England, in October 1945. Tigy was adamant that Boule should be left behind, or she would not go with her husband. Simenon saw that he would lose his son if the couple parted, so he gave in to his wife's wishes. But Tigy's demand left him more discontent than ever with their relationship and would have consequences once they were living on the other side of the Atlantic.

After ten days in New York, visiting Georges's publisher and other French ex-pats, the Simenons headed north and rented accommodation in Canada, in French-speaking Montreal. Simenon needed a bilingual secretary and interviewed nearly two hundred applicants, but could not find what he was looking for. It was one of his Canadian publishers who recommended a French-Canadian, Denyse Ouimet, who was currently working in the States but was thinking of returning home. Simenon met her for lunch in Manhattan in November, exactly one month to the day after he and Tigy had landed in New York, and they become lovers that evening.

Simenon was at an emotionally vulnerable stage in his life, all certainties swept aside by the war and its aftermath. He fell madly in love with Denyse, to the point of being demented with a desire he had never felt for any woman before. Denyse was mercurial, flirtatious and sexy. She was a woman of the world and had some experience of men. Simenon believed he was protecting a vulnerable young woman from a harsh world; Denyse saw their affair as an adventure and would often talk of previous lovers, causing him to be violently jealous. Tigy did not sense the depth of their passion until Georges fell ill after making love to Denyse in the snow and he insisted that his secretary nurse him.

The *ménage à trois* seemed to work for a while but, after Simenon set off for a tour of the States with Denyse in 1946, Tigy decided Boule should join them in their new home in Arizona in 1948. This was probably a deliberate ploy on Tigy's part to put the cat among the pigeons, but it was all too late, for Denyse was not the type to be jealous of anyone. And, soon, she was pregnant.

When Georges asked his wife for a divorce so that he could marry Denyse, Tigy told him there would come a moment when he would want consolation from her. It was a remark he would often recall in the turbulent years that followed. But, whereas Boule was devastated by the news that Denyse was carrying Simenon's child, and not she, Tigy remained level-headed and focused. She found a slick divorce lawyer who made it clear that Georges was not in a position to duck his responsibilities. Tigy came away with an income for life, their house in France and the furniture, along with their collection of valuable Impressionist paintings. She also took all of her husband's shares and had only to agree, in return, to live with Marc within six miles of Simenon's home. Since Boule remained with Tigy and Marc, Georges was able to keep his harem around him, even if he was a lot poorer than before.

It was Denyse who reacted to her future husband's divorce settlement. In the end, Simenon left her with his lawyer to hammer out the details while he looked after his new son, John, who had arrived in September 1949. By June the following year, everyone was resettled in Carmel, California and the divorce went ahead. Georges was given his freedom in the courthouse at Reno, Nevada, on 21 June 1950. The following day, on 22 June, the writer re-entered the courthouse building and married Denyse. After the ceremony, the bride walked her new husband to a nearby fountain and, at her suggestion, Georges threw his old wedding ring into the water. He had been strangely depressed before the ceremony, and now his thoughts turned again to his beloved Europe.

But Simenon could see it was not a good time to leave America. The knock-on effect of the Korean War in 1950 had caused a flood of applications by Europeans hoping to settle in the United States. The writer decided, instead, to buy a house in the country where he could work in peace, just as he had in the Vendée during the war. The eighteenth century house the couple found in Lakeville, Connecticut, came with fifty acres of woods and the only mortgage Georges ever took out, but he was flat broke after his divorce and could only rent a home in nearby Salmon Creek for Tigy, Boule and Marc. The next five years were some of his most productive and, perhaps, the last time he was truly content. He wrote thirteen Maigrets and fourteen other novels while he was there and built up a magnificent reference library. To crown his happiness, his adored daughter, Marie-Jo, was born in 1953. Simenon began to feel like a regular American family man, watching TV with a beer, his children growing up in the big outdoors. Denyse became an outstanding secretary and personal assistant. His book sales topped three million a year and around thirty million novels, in all. He became president of the Mystery Writers of America in 1952, lectured at Yale and made friends with other writers. But still, in the back of his mind, Europe beckoned.

His first trip 'home' was in 1952, when he was treated like a movie star: followed everywhere by the press and fans of his work. He had become so famous that he and his family needed police protection. The razzmatazz caught Denyse by surprise; she'd had no idea how famous her husband was. In Belgium, he was received into the Royal Belgian Academy, but not by the King, as the writer was a divorcé. It was, perhaps, to be expected that Georges's mother would not hit it off with his new wife, since both women had strong characters and a forthright manner.

Back in Connecticut, the family prospered, although Georges's preoccupation with his daughter soon led to an overheated relationship that was to have disastrous consequences. Simenon felt the need to protect his little girl from life's setbacks. He believed she needed constant love and affection, just as he did. When she was only a few months old, he rushed by her pram one day, forgetting to stop and talk to her. The child went into a state of shock until he spoke to her and brought her round. Georges saw this as confirmation of his daughter's acute sensibility. When Boule left Tigy and returned to the Simenon household, the writer began to think seriously about becoming a US citizen.

But McCarthyism was sweeping America and Simenon's fellow Mystery Writer, Dashiell Hammett, was sent to prison for refusing to testify before the Committee. Simenon smelled the fear among his colleagues and heard their silence. He had seen similar 'witch hunts' in war-torn Europe and lost his desire to become an American. Besides, something strange had happened to Denyse's behaviour since the birth of their daughter. He would catch her out in tall stories about her past and she began to be jealous of Simenon's life before he'd met her. She became obsessed with her weight and, after being bitten by lice in a down-market hotel they were obliged to stay in one night, she would scrub clean and disinfect any hotel room they slept in. Was it stress or post-natal depression? Or was Denyse simply fed up with the life she was leading? It was clear she was unhappy at home, unable to communicate with her husband, and spent time drinking in bars. Ever since their trip to Europe in 1952, when Georges had been feted as a celebrity writer, she had longed to live on this welcoming continent. On the advice of his doctor, Georges took Denyse on trips to New York, hoping these would divert her.

When his publisher asked him why he lived in the United States, Simenon began to ask himself the same question. With his usual impulsiveness, he decided it was time to move again. He told himself that a return to Europe would make his wife happy once more. Tigy was delighted to be going home; she had never really settled in America, and Boule was happy to follow the family, wherever they went.

First stop, in March 1955, was Paris but the family soon moved south to a house near Cannes. Denyse suffered a miscarriage and Georges took her on a tour of France, thinking they might find a permanent place to live. They found nothing. Not long after, Somerset Maugham came to lunch and the two writers of popular fiction shared the usual gripes about sniffy critics, begging letters and, significantly, how to avoid taxes.

That Georges and Denyse were not getting along was obvious, even to five year-old Johnny Simenon. The boy would have liked to have returned to America and the happy times they'd had there. But several factors combined to send the family in another direction. It was to be Simenon's last port of call and the end of his marriage to Denyse.

Switzerland was an attractive place for the Simenons to live for a number of reasons: the couple loved the hillside city of Lausanne, looking out across Lake Geneva to the French town of Evian and the Alps beyond, and their children would receive an education of the highest quality and in more than one language. But it was the tax system that really attracted Simenon, always the businessman. In 1957, Denyse and Georges took slow and extensive taxi tours of Lausanne and its surrounding villages, looking for the perfect house to buy. Having found none they liked, they took a lease that summer on the Château d'Echandens, just outside Lausanne. Here, the writer rolled up his sleeves again and got down to work, in spite of his deteriorating family life, or because of it.

As if to compensate for the downward spiral of their relationship, the Simenons went shopping in style, and could now afford to do so. Denyse stocked up at Cartier, Hermès and Lanvin while Georges bought a Chrysler and a Rolls Royce by cheque at the Geneva motor show. Their home was impressive: behind the tall gates and railings was a gothic castle in miniature with turrets, outbuildings and parkland overlooking Lausanne and the lake beyond. They lived the high life and employed a squad of servants to keep the château running smoothly. Denyse had two secretaries of her own and Boule was there to cook for them. In addition to Denyse and Boule, Simenon struck up physical relationships with several of the maids. But it was to be in 1961, when Georges and Denyse engaged a thirty-four year-old Italian housemaid, Teresa Sburelin, that the writer would begin his last important affair. For Teresa would become Georges's 'rock' in his final years.

The Simenon's last child, Pierre, was born in May 1959, but the birth did not repair the marriage. At Cannes, during Simenon's presidency of the Film Festival in 1960, they rubbed shoulders with brilliant movie makers, such as Fellini, but the change of scenery did little to improve Denyse's disposition. Simenon was still sexually demanding but his wife appeared to be fed up with his persistent manner. Her terseness began to kill the last spark of affection he had for her. He tried taking her for drives, he tried piling on the drinks to revive the fervour in which their relationship had caught fire. But drink induced quarrels, rather than romance. One evening when the couple were fighting, Simenon rang for the doctor to give Denyse an injection to calm her down, but the doctor gave the injection to Georges, instead.

Denyse regarded her husband's relationship with Teresa, their new Venetian maid, as normal practice in their household. She would disappear into her offices with her secretaries while Simenon, when he wasn't writing, would focus on his children, especially his daughter, the fragile Marie-Jo. When Georges and Denyse made a trip to London in 1962, Teresa went with them. A few months later, Denyse spent the first of several periods at a clinic in Prangins, near Nyon.

At first, Georges felt lost without his regular sparring partner. But the construction of a motorway close to the château prompted a decision to move house again, and his mind was occupied for a while. He bought a large plot of meadowland at Epalinges, high above Lausanne, with a spectacular view of the lake and the Alps. The house was designed by an architect to the Simenons' specification: a large ranch-style mansion with plenty of space for all the family and their friends. But, by the time the huge white building was completed in 1963, the marriage was virtually over. After one of Denyse's visits to the clinic, Simenon stood at the door of their new home and prevented his wife from entering, telling her, with tears in his eyes, that she should return to the clinic. Denyse was to live at Epalinges for only four months.

But others were welcome at the mansion. Charlie Chaplin, Georges's neighbour in nearby Corsier-sur-Vevey, enjoyed visiting the writer's new home. The house was impressive in size and content: six washing machines and a full-time laundress were employed in the central laundry, fed by chutes from the bedrooms. There were over twenty main rooms and a servants' wing with its own dining room for the staff. A listening system was installed in many of the rooms, so that Simenon could listen out for the children, and a complex layout of corridors, with identical portraits of Simenon on the walls, often confused guests. Simenon's routine never varied: rising at dawn, checking over the house and its utilities, the long walk, lunch with Marie-Jo facing him at the other end of the table, the business calls and bed early with a glass or two of whisky.

Simenon, like many writers, needed his routine and rituals, and the children soon learned that their father needed absolute quiet when he was writing a novel. When Denyse finally left the marital home in April 1964, Simenon rattled around the big complex, and his mood swings often puzzled and frightened the children: one minute he was the strict father, bent on teaching them the value of money, the next he was magnanimous to the point of over-indulgence. Not many months after Denyse's departure, he ordered a tearful Boule to leave. She and Teresa were not getting along and, after thirty-nine years of service in the Simenon household, the faithful housekeeper went to live with Georges's oldest son, Marc, and his young family.

Once Boule had left, Teresa took centre stage as the woman in Simenon's life. One night in 1965, the writer fell on his bathroom floor and broke several of his ribs. Teresa heard his call for help and got him to the hospital in Lausanne, where she slept beside his bed and watched over him constantly. She would remain quietly at the side of her 'monsieur' for the rest of his life.

The Swiss magazine, *Médecine et Hygiène*, arranged for a group of five doctors to visit the writer for an article on his working methods. Simenon told them how he moved from his own persona to that of his main character, often using a domestic odour to evoke a situation, such as the smell of clean sheets in the linen cupboard at Epalinges. The doctors noted, however, how organised the building seemed and lacking in homely smells. The truth was that Simenon had little idea how he embarked upon a new story. He knew it was not a facility he could switch on and off at will. He had to wait for the muse to visit him and, sometimes, life got in the way and blocked her path. Like Dickens, he knew his imagination was connected to demons in his past, his childhood experiences. It is no coincidence that, when his mother died, so did Georges's urge to tell stories.

Simenon's mother visited the mansion in Epalinges in 1967, full of anxiety that her son had fallen into debt in maintaining such a vast place. In 1969, her health failing, she moved to an old people's home in Liège where she died in 1970. When Georges arrived at her deathbed, the old lady's memory failing, she could only ask why he had come. It seemed to Simenon that his mother had rejected him right up to the end. Emotionally spent, he could not write for a whole year. In 1971, he wrote his last novel, and his last 'Maigret' was completed in February 1972.

Soon after that, Georges quit the big house at Epalinges and moved to an eighth floor apartment in the centre of Lausanne. There, he turned to dictating his memoirs into a tape machine: twenty-one volumes of reminiscences, detailed accounts of his past. A year later, in 1974, feeling uncomfortable in the apartment, he moved again, with Teresa and his youngest son, Pierre, to a nearby terraced house in Avenue des Figuiers. Two months after he'd installed himself in this modest setting, a home as unpretentious as the one he'd grown up in, he dictated his famous *Lettre à ma mère* in which he tried to deal with his guilt over his troubled relationship with his mother.

With Henriette, his mother, no longer causing him emotional pain, Simenon directed his ire towards his estranged wife. The couple's battles continued in print and particularly affected Marie-Jo, who loved both her parents. Psychologically fragile, she took it badly when her mother told her daughter about Simenon's relationship with Teresa. Marie-Jo could accept her mother being intimate with her father, but no other woman. The girl saw herself as her father's other love. She had even asked him, as a girl, to buy her a wedding ring, which she wore for the rest of her short life.

After leaving school, Marie-Jo went to Paris where she tried to make a life of her own. But her adoration for her father remained; at least two of her relationships were with men who seemed to be father-figures. Her attempts to be a singer and an actress in Paris were not successful. In addition, she was upset that there was no room for her in the small house Simenon now shared with Teresa. Six times, the distraught young woman tried to commit suicide. The seventh attempt was on 20 May 1978, one month after Denyse Simenon published her account of her marriage to Georges. Marie-Jo had read the book and seen the publicity on French television. After a last phone call to her father, she took a rifle and shot herself through the heart. Simenon was devastated. Marie-Jo's ashes were scattered under the old cedar tree in the writer's back garden in Lausanne.

Tigy, Simenon's first wife, never remarried and, in 1985, she sold her house in France and went to live with her son, Marc, and his family. She died with hardly a word of recrimination over the way Simenon had treated her. Denyse repeatedly asked Georges for a divorce, but the writer was against the idea as it would have cost him a substantial part of his fortune. She then moved to France and became a qualified and experienced psychoanalyst before returning to Nyon in Switzerland, not far from the clinic at Prangins where she had been staying when her marriage collapsed.

Teresa devoted her life to pleasing Simenon in any way she could. He required her to sit with him when he was dictating, but she was not allowed to read a book of her own lest her page-turning disturb his concentration. If she wanted to read, she had to wait until Simenon was asleep, then steal into the bathroom to turn her pages. They lived on, under Simenon's exacting daily routine, in the little house in Lausanne for fifteen years. In 1984, the author underwent brain surgery and recovered with Teresa's care. He remained alert until the end, although he spent the last year of his life in a wheelchair. He did not complain.

After falling from his bed, Georges Simenon died in the early hours of the morning on 4 September 1989. He was cremated just a stone's throw from the little house, in the crematorium at Montoie where he'd often walked in the gardens. His children learned of his death only when they heard about it on the radio. Simenon had wanted to spare them the obligation of gathering for his end, and left instructions for Teresa to scatter his ashes under the old cedar tree where he had dispersed Marie-Jo's, eleven years earlier.

Teresa lived on in their modest house in Lausanne with an income Georges had left her. She never spoke publicly about her relationship with Simenon, nor did she open her house to the press. Simenon's estate was shared between Denyse and his remaining children. Apart from his millions in world royalties and his collection of Impressionist paintings, he left apartments in Lausanne and the ranch at Epalinges, now bordered by newly-built villas.

One day, when Simenon and his old friend, Charlie Chaplin, were comparing begging letters, they discovered they had received mail from the same Italian woman pleading poverty and an overlarge family to support. Simenon's decision to be cremated brought to an end his being viewed by others as a source of instant cash, whereas his friend, Chaplin, continued to be seen as a valuable commodity, even after his death.

Chapter 2

Charlie Chaplin

T he spade met a solid object with a thud and the man grunted. He couldn't see much in the dark, rain pelting his face, shoes sodden, rivulets of water pouring into the hole they'd dug, but he knew he'd struck gold. He lifted his head and gave a low whistle. His partner, shovelling clods of mud at the other end of the grave, stopped digging immediately and scrambled over the wet earth to join him.

'C'est ça? The coffin? *C'est Charlot?'*

The other man nodded and wiped his face, then he gave his companion a shove. 'Hurry,' he hissed. 'We've taken too long already. My fingers are numb, my feet are like ice – '

'I didn't change the plan,' the other protested. 'It wasn't my idea! This is madness – '

'Shut up!' growled his companion. 'Someone will hear us. Get back to work!'

'I still think we should leave him here,' the other man mumbled as he crawled back across the muddy pile. 'We can bury him deep. They'll think he's gone – '

'I said, shut up and dig!' came the terse reply. 'We do it my way, Gantcho. I'm the boss! You want to be rich, don't you?'

The other said nothing and began digging again. Suddenly he stood up, leaned on his shovel and looked back at his boss with a frown. 'You know, Roman, they didn't have this trouble with the Italian body, that industrialist – '

'They didn't have this damn weather,' Roman squinted at the night sky with exasperation, then at Gantcho. 'You still want that garage, don't you? Our own business, like we said?'

'Yes, but – '

'Then let's get this box in the back of the car before someone hears us, or sees us!'

It took Roman and Gantcho another half hour to uncover the casket. The rain was unceasing, slashing at their backs as they worked. At last, they threw their shovels aside and grasped the handles of the coffin. It wouldn't budge. They looked at each other. They tried again.

'It must be full of rocks!'

'Stupid! He's lined with lead, that's all!'

'We can't move it! Not all the way through the cemetery! Not on a night like this – '

'Yes, we can! When I say lift, we lift! Now, one, two, three ... '

With all their strength, the two men hauled the oblong box out of the hole and dragged it, in a zigzag fashion, along the waterlogged path. Two or three times, their feet skidded beneath them, gouging the neat pathway. Once, the coffin slipped from their hands altogether and landed on the ground with a muffled thump. Finally, they reached the cemetery gates. Gantcho ran to the car, opened the tailgate and hurried back to help with the casket. 'Where are we going to keep him, Roman?' he panted as they pushed and pulled the coffin into the back of the car. 'We'd better make the call tonight – '

'Shut up! When I say so, not before! We do it right! We're talking big bucks here. I got an idea for Charlie. Now, get ready ... one, two, three – !'

Hannah Chaplin sighed as she led her two sons towards the workhouse gates. This was not how she'd thought it would be. Life had gone horribly wrong for her in the last few years. She had left home as a young girl with hope in her heart. She had been pretty and talented, or so she thought. But life on the stage had been hard. Why, young Charlie had turned out to be a better entertainer than she was. She glanced down at the mop-headed nine year-old holding her hand and skipping along beside her. His older brother, Sydney, wore a more thoughtful look as he walked down Renfrew Road with reluctant steps. But, then, Syd knew more about life inside the workhouse than Charlie; he knew what lay ahead of them. This would not be the first time the Chaplins had needed charity in order to survive.

Hannah had done her best to keep them together. She had tried every sort of employment. Just about everything. But now, even her men friends had deserted her. Poverty had robbed her of her looks. The last lover had left and taken their son with him; told her she wasn't fit to be a mother. That had crushed her. From then on, it was one setback after another. And now she had no spirit left to fight, to find work for herself, food for her sons, enough money to pay the rent. Their clothes were rags, their shoes beyond repair, their stomachs ached with hunger.

The three of them stood in front of the grey building and gazed up at its dark windows. A gaunt man, with greasy hair hanging in slats on his grubby coat, limped towards the gates and swung them open. Hannah led the boys into the shadowy courtyard. Charlie ceased to skip. He looked up at his mother and gripped her hand as tightly as he could. Hannah smiled wanly, trying to uncurl the small, thin fingers from her own. 'Here, Syd,' she said in a low voice. 'Be a good boy and take Charlie with you. We'll meet up. Always do, don't we? Look after yerself and the little 'un. Be good and say your prayers. Pray they find your father and get him to send us some money. Lord knows we need it. Lord knows we've done our best. There, now; don't cry, our Charles. Wipe yer tears, ducks. You go along with Syd. I'm going the other way, up them steps. The Lord will provide.'

Hannah Hill was born to a poor cobbler, Charles Hill, in South London in 1865. Her mother, Mary Anne Hill, gave birth to a second daughter, Kate, in 1870. But the couple and their two girls, as well as Mary Ann's son by her first husband, a sign writer who had fallen from a horse-drawn bus and cracked his skull and died, lived in dire circumstances, though Mrs Hill tried to help her husband with his business. And it was not only economic hardship that had made the family's life miserable. Charles and Mary Ann did not get on together and they argued constantly. It was said that Mary Ann had been unfaithful, that she had been caught out by her husband. Whatever caused the problem, the marriage did not last and Mary Ann moved out to lodge with a couple of women a few streets away. To provide for herself, she sold second-hand clothes in the street. Unfortunately, she spent what little money she earned on gin. In 1893, she collapsed with the D.T.s and was declared insane and taken to the County Asylum.

From this unpromising beginning, Hannah tried to make her way in the world. She left home as soon as she could and took her younger sister with her. Both girls were pretty and stage-struck, and probably had gentlemen friends to support them. By the time Hannah met Charles Spencer Chaplin, a promising young music hall singer, she was living at her uncle's home in Brandon Street with her baby son, Sydney. Hannah always maintained that Sydney had been the result of a romantic elopement to South Africa with a certain Mr Hawkes. But this gentleman had long since disappeared by the time Hannah married Charles in 1885, fourteen weeks after the birth of Sydney.

The late nineteenth century was a vibrant period for the British music hall, and Lambeth in South London was a hub of the business. Agents and artistes based themselves in the area and met up in Kennington and Brixton pubs on a Sunday morning. Twenty-two year-old Charles and his new bride were well-placed to become stage successes. But Hannah's career faltered just as Charles's began to take off. With the stage name Lily Harley, she played some venues in the provinces at the bottom of the bill. Charles began as a mimic and soon developed into a dramatic singer, specialising in songs about domestic strife. He could sing from experience, too, since his drinking fuelled a violent temper and Hannah would leave the family home, just as her mother had done. By the time Charlie was born, on 16 April 1889, Charles Senior was appearing in a successful show in Hull, in the north of England, and Hannah's career had collapsed.

Charlie always maintained he had been born in Walworth, South London, and that, soon after his birth, the family had moved to much smarter lodgings due to his father's earning power. But part of the duties of a music hall star was to drink with his customers in the bar after the show. Chaplin Senior's habit of rolling home late and drunk did nothing to help the marriage, or his alcoholism. By the time he toured the United States in 1890, one year after Charlie was born, his marriage to Hannah was over. A year later, Hannah was enjoying an affair with a music hall singer who often shared the bill with her husband. George Dryden Wheeler, who sang under the stage name of Leo Dryden, had a violent temper equal to that of Charles Chaplin. In 1892, Hannah gave birth to Wheeler's son, George Dryden, named after his father, and, for a while, they all lived comfortably, funded by Dryden. But the relationship deteriorated and Dryden left Hannah, taking their six month-old child with him. This must have devastated Hannah, who now had to provide for Sydney and Charlie without any support from her estranged husband, Chaplin, or her ex-lover, Wheeler. The good times, such as they had been, were over for Hannah, Sydney and Charlie. But the many hardships they would suffer would forge a bond between the brothers that would last for the rest of their lives.

From then on, the family often moved lodgings, possibly to avoid paying rent that was due. Although Hannah was a loving mother and adored by her sons, their hand to mouth existence, the stress of not knowing where the next meal would come from, began to affect her health. She tried to keep up their spirits by enacting routines from her music hall days, which delighted Sydney and Charlie and inspired them, later on, to make their careers on the stage. On a practical level, she tried to claim support from Chaplin Senior but he rarely sent the family any money. His own career was on the slide and his health was no longer good. He had taken up with another woman and they had a child of their own. Hannah tried to return to the stage but her nerves had been affected by malnutrition and rough lodgings. When Charlie was still a child, she was engaged to sing at a venue in Aldershot. During her turn, she lost her voice and the audience, mostly soldiers from the barracks, turned on her and became abusive. Charlie always said this moment became his first appearance on the stage: the manager, who had watched the child doing little routines to amuse people backstage, pushed the boy onto the boards in an effort to placate the audience. Charlie sang a music hall number and the crowd was delighted. They threw coins onto the stage and Charlie, knowing how much the family needed money, told the audience he would give them another song, just as soon as he'd picked up the money.

But it wasn't always so easy to earn a crust. Hannah and the boys never knew from one day to the next whether they would eat or starve. She took in sewing, working by candlelight, long into the night, until the company who supplied her with items to repair repossessed her sewing machine when she fell behind with the payments. It was to her credit that Hannah kept the family together as long as she did. She turned to religion and the routines with which she entertained her boys in their shabby digs took a biblical turn. The boys found it less amusing when they were mocked by other children because of their ill-fitting clothes. Hannah had no money for winter coats or socks and made garments for the boys from scraps of cast-offs. But no matter how she economised, no matter how she went without, the stress of trying to survive on next to nothing finally broke her.

In 1895, Hannah began to suffer from blinding headaches that Charlie would later call migraines. She was admitted to Lambeth Infirmary where she remained for a whole month. Charlie boarded with a relative and Sydney was taken to the local workhouse where, after four days, he was sent to a school for the poor in West Norwood. After that, he lodged with Charles Chaplin Senior until Hannah was strong enough to take Sydney back. But, the following year, Hannah had another breakdown and was sent to Champion Hill Infirmary. This time, both Charlie and Sydney were sent to a workhouse, at Newington, then on to the Poor Law school in rural Hanwell, not far from London. The school was well-run and clean, with the accent on health and education. But Charlie, now aged seven, had experienced enough disruption in his formative years to affect him for the rest of his life. Later on, the pathos of his tramp character, the ill-fitting clothes, the battle against authority, the struggle to survive against overwhelming odds, the lot of the underdog: all these were situations that had already marked young Charlie; experiences he knew about, first-hand.

Sydney was given the opportunity to train for the navy and Charlie was left alone in the institution at Hanwell until his mother was well enough to visit him, fourteen months later. She now felt able to take the boys home and Charles Senior had been tracked down and threatened with jail if he did not support his family. Yet again, the payments stopped and, in 1898, Hannah had no alternative but to lead her boys to the Lambeth workhouse where they were separated, once again. Whilst there, they were reunited for one memorable day when she engineered an outing for the three of them in the park. Then it was back to the workhouse. Not long after that, Hannah was transferred to Lambeth Infirmary again, her whole body, for some mysterious reason, covered in bruises. One week later, she was admitted to Cane Hill Asylum, near Redhill in Surrey. Her frenzied behaviour, possibly brought on by stress or, perhaps, schizophrenia or as one doctor believed, syphilis, caused the nurses and doctors to confine her to a padded cell.

Now Chaplin Senior had no choice but to accept responsibility for Charlie and Sydney. The boys were sent to live with him in his two rooms in Kennington Road. But their father's common-in-law wife, Louise, resented the boys' presence from the start. She had a young son of her own by Charlie's father, as well as an alcohol problem almost as acute as that of Chaplin Senior. This made boarding with the couple and their child a tense, over-crowded affair and, almost immediately, there was particular conflict between Sydney and Louise. When his father was in a good mood, Charlie would enjoy the once-popular entertainer's renditions of his music hall acts. But drunken violence was in the air, and Louise and Charles Senior would frequently come to blows. Charlie, himself, was often locked out of the home. This prompted a visit by the Society for the Prevention of Cruelty to Children, but the two months during which the brothers lodged with Chaplin seemed to them to drag on for much longer than that.

Hannah had recovered sufficiently from her illness by November 1898 to retrieve her boys and she found them a room behind a pickle factory, the odour from which permeated the air for several streets around. The lodging was also next to a slaughterhouse where Charlie witnessed a tragi-comic scene that would influence the stories he would later create for the screen. A sheep, on its way to be killed, broke free and was chased through the streets while people hooted with laughter. The boy could see the grim side of the chase, the sense of a living creature fighting for its freedom against all odds.

Life was not particularly pleasant at the back of the pickle factory but Chaplin Senior was making enough of a financial contribution to keep the Board of Guardians from arresting him. Sydney got a job as a telegraph boy at the Post Office and Hannah took in sewing again. Charlie was sent back to school to continue his much-interrupted education but, to his relief, in 1898, when he was ten years old, his father found him work with a group of clog dancers called The Eight Lancashire Lads. Young Charlie was an intelligent boy with an inquiring mind, but learning by rote in the classroom had killed his interest in academic study. He was supposed to continue his education at schools in various towns where the troupe played. It was only later, when he felt financially secure, that Charlie would worry about the paucity of his knowledge.

The troupe played the Victorian music halls at the height of their popularity. Charlie watched other turns from the wings and learned a great deal. He loved to mimic different acts, especially the tragic scenes from Dickens. At one point the management gave him a solo spot but the crowd whistled and stamped and booed him. It taught the ten year-old how to engage with an audience and during his two years with the group he gained valuable experience in pantomime. In *Cinderella*, he took his role of the pantomime cat to heart. Although the audience loved his improvisation, he was soon informed by the management that a cat who sniffed a dog and raised its leg against the scenery was not required, and nor would he be, if he continued.

It was a damp morning on 1st March 1978 when Monsieur Etienne Buenzod, superintendent of the cemetery at Corsier-sur-Vevey in Switzerland, made his way along the avenue of headstones that led to Charlie Chaplin's grave. It had rained hard in the night but the chilly morning mist had finally begun to clear and Monsieur Buenzod could almost see the tops of the mountains on the other side of Lake Geneva. He was peering so intently at the Dents du Midi that he nearly fell into a large hole where Chaplin had been laid to rest, nine weeks earlier. He pulled up sharply. He stared. He rubbed his eyes and stared again; he scratched his head. He couldn't believe Charlot's coffin had disappeared. He walked around the empty plot, first one way, then the other. He raised his arms heavenwards. Nothing like this had ever happened in Switzerland before.

Who would have done such a thing? Buenzod pondered. Dug up the corpse of the greatest comedian the world had ever known? The press would have a field day with this, he was sure. Was it a souvenir hunter with a taste for the macabre? Or one of Charlie's legions of fans across the globe? Was it a group who suspected that Charlot had really been of Jewish stock? Or were neo-Nazis remembering his portrayal of Hitler in *The Great Dictator*? Whatever had occurred, this was a matter for the police. But what would Lady Chaplin say when they told her Sir Charles's body was missing? Monsieur Buenzod hurried back along the avenue, still shaking his head in disbelief, forgetting all about the view of the lake and the majestic mountains beyond.

Young Charlie loved the stage, but touring with the clog dancing team was hard work and his mother saw her son grow pale and thin. Sydney's naval training enabled him to get work on the mail run to the Cape. He was a good worker and soon became a steward and a ship's bandsman, and the money he sent home allowed Hannah to move the family into two rooms over a barber's shop. Now living back in Lambeth, Charlie happened to catch sight of his father, one day in 1901, in a pub on the Kennington Road. The twelve year-old was shaken by his father's appearance. Chaplin Senior was frail and emotional. He took his son in his arms and kissed him. His father had never done anything like that before. It was clear the man was dying. At thirty-seven years old, Charles Chaplin Senior had cirrhosis of the liver and dropsy. He had only a few weeks to live. He and Hannah ceased their warring and Chaplin died in St Thomas's Hospital in May 1901. Like Georges Simenon's family, Hannah had no money with which to bury her husband. Unlike Simenon's relatives, one of Charlie's uncles, who had made good in South Africa, volunteered to pay the funeral expenses. The funeral party went on to a sumptuous lunch, after dropping Hannah and Charlie back at their lodgings where there was no food or money to buy something to eat.

Sydney's wages at sea were a help to the family. They moved to Pownall Terrace, Kennington Road: an attic lodging that would figure more than any other in Charlie's film work. Having left school permanently, the boy tried to earn money in a variety of ways. Wearing the black arm band he had been given to mourn his father, he assumed a pathetic air and sold flowers in the Lambeth pubs. When his mother disapproved of that, he became a barber's boy, then worked for a chandler. He became a doctors' boy, but was sacked because he was too short to clean the practice's long windows. One of the doctors took pity on him and gave him a job as a page in the family home. But the doctor's wife caught him, one day, using a piece of drainpipe as an alpenhorn, and he had to go. W.H. Smith sacked him for being under age. He was a one-day wonder in a glass factory. His efforts at feeding a printing press at the stationers, Strakers, would not have been out of place in his film *Modern Times*. He took all the old clothes he could find in the attic room in Pownall Terrace and sold them on the pavement, hoping to make as much money as the stall holders he had seen in Petticoat Lane. He made very little. Then he helped two Scotsmen make penny toys in a mews behind Kennington Road and decided to set up in business for himself. It was only when his mother was overwhelmed by the smell of glue in their garret that he was forced to try his hand at something else.

Then, in 1903, disaster struck. Sydney was still away at sea when Charlie, returning home one day, saw a knot of children hanging around the front door to their lodgings. As soon as they saw him, they shouted to him that his mother had gone mad. Charlie was already aware that Hannah was slipping into another crisis: she had stopped sewing and caring for herself and cleaning their small room. Now, she was knocking on the doors of neighbours and giving them pieces of coal as birthday presents. Charlie was upset, embarrassed and fearful as he led his staggering mother to the Lambeth Infirmary. The doctors accounted for Hannah's shouting and screaming and religious utterances as the result of malnutrition. Apart from a short spell when she seemed to rally, Hannah Chaplin would spend the next seven and a half years in Cane Hill mental hospital.

Now Charlie was on his own, living a hand to mouth existence. Some woodchoppers took pity on him and gave him some work. They took him to see the great Fred Karno's Speechless Comedians: a troupe that would soon play an important part in his career. When Syd returned home and they visited their mother in Cane Hill, it was clear the boys would have to manage their own lives. It was Syd who first suggested they become actors, but it was Charlie who became one first.

Stan Laurel, a former Fred Karno actor, would later remember Charlie Chaplin as a timid fellow who had the courage to take comedy to new heights. In spite of his natural reticence, the little fellow did the rounds of theatrical agents and wouldn't take no for an answer. Finally, in 1903, at the age of fourteen, his perseverance paid off and he was offered the role of a page boy in a Sherlock Holmes drama. Syd, who had yet to break into the business, helped his brother learn his lines and generally played the role of manager until Charlie found him a part in the play. Charlie was beginning to realise that his lack of education could seriously hamper his reading for parts. The play toured the country and received good notices. Charlie learned as much stagecraft as he could. He bought a camera and did his own processing and developing. His life was already moving in the direction of films. But his childhood experiences had taught him to be careful with money and he always would be, in spite of the fabulous sums he would earn. He would need security, too, as his path to success would not be a straightforward one.

It was Sydney who first landed a job with Fred Karno's troupe, the popular comedy group. Syd had gone back to sea to earn some money and discovered his talent for comedy in concerts on board ship. He returned home and he and Charlie became comedians in different shows. Charlie soon picked up the technique of burlesque. Syd secured a contract with Fred Karno's international touring companies in 1906. It took him a while to persuade his boss to give Charlie a job but, in February 1908, Charlie left Casey's Circus and joined Sydney in pantomime, burlesque, circus and music hall sketches with the top names of the day. Karno had ten touring companies, both at home and abroad. Charlie could hardly believe his luck when he went with a troupe to Paris. Now the brothers were able to move to their first comfortable home, in upper class Brixton, and furnish it with some exotic pieces of furniture.

Charlie loved women; very young women. Like his fellow actors, he was happy to enjoy the local brothel when the company rolled into town, and Paris was no exception to that. But, for him, young girls had an irresistible appeal, a certain innocence in a world Charlie knew was tough and grasping. At Streatham Empire in 1908, he fell madly in love with a chorus girl on the same bill: Hetty Kelly. But his ardent courtship of the girl frightened the fifteen year-old and her mother told him to stay away. He would idolise Hetty in his memory, her place in his heart assured when she died young. But it was a pattern of romancing Charlie would repeat far too often for his own good and would land him in serious trouble.

The phone rang twice before Geraldine Chaplin picked up the receiver. She took a deep breath. 'Yes?' Her voice sounded hesitant, slightly afraid.

'You got the note?'

'Yes.' She almost said thank you, out of politeness. She was a well-brought up young woman. Her father had insisted on that.

'You are one of the family, *non*?'

'I'm Monsieur Chaplin's eldest daughter. My mother is too ill with the stress of what has happened to come to the phone.'

'Ah.' The man seemed satisfied with this explanation and took a moment to savour it.

'Please!' Geraldine sobbed, 'Wherever you have my father, is he safe?'

The man grunted. 'Safe enough. For the moment. But you must pay us soon.'

'We don't have the money! We can't pay you – '

'Don't lie to me! I know that isn't true!'

'But six hundred thousand Swiss francs is – '

'The papers say your mother has twelve million pounds in her bank account now.'

Geraldine gave a helpless whimper. 'That's the press! They say these things! Oh, please, be careful with my father's body!'

There was a pause the other end. Geraldine could hear the roar of traffic in the background. The call had to be from a public phone box. That made sense. 'I tell you what,' the man sounded confident now, in control of the situation. 'I'm a generous person. My partner is, too. Call it half a million; discount for prompt payment – ' The wail of an ambulance siren drowned out the rest of his sentence.

'But we don't have that sort of money in cash!' Geraldine pleaded. 'My mother, she's so ill - !' Too late; the line went dead. She replaced the receiver and looked across to where the policeman was sitting. A broad grin stole across her face. 'How was that, Superintendent?'

'*Parfait, madame. Vraiment parfait,*' replied Monsieur Gabriel Cettou, chief of the Geneva police. 'You are an excellent actress, *c'est sûr.* A credit to your profession. Tell Lady Chaplin we will have these dolts behind bars very soon. Jules, did you trace that number? *On y va!*'

In September 1910, Charlie Chaplin and Stan Laurel, among others, sailed to the United States of America for their first music hall tour. Sydney was on another of Karno's tours, in England. The older Chaplin brother was a talented comedian, in Karno's opinion, and too valuable to be lured by American vaudeville, never to return home. Charlie was another consideration. He was not well liked in the company. His natural shyness gave others the impression he was cold and stand-offish. And for some reason, best known to himself, he kept away from the bars and didn't stand a round. He was careful with money and put as much of his salary as possible into the bank. He seemed moody. He would read books instead of making conversation. He would dress like a poor man one minute, then astound his colleagues by decking himself out in expensive clothes the next. Charlie was complex. He could be anything he wanted to be. He was a chameleon, a first-class actor.

At first, Chaplin wasn't sure he liked America. He found the pace of life in New York a little frightening. But, soon enough, the opportunity of making a fast buck energised him. By the time the American tour ended in 1912, Charlie had made some friends and become a success on the stage with his name on the Karno playbills. When he returned to England, he and Syd were able to have their mother transferred to a home in Peckham. But Syd had married a Karno actress, Minnie Constance, while Charlie was away and London now had less appeal for Charlie than the United States. He signed for a second U.S. Karno tour, but soon found he was bored with the same old routines in the same hick towns. He was saving and investing as much as he could and already had one eye on the burgeoning silent movie industry. He knew he could reach a much larger audience by acting in the 'flickers'. In November 1913, he left Fred Karno and signed a contract with the Keystone Film Studio in California, run by Mack Sennett.

Keystone comedies were short and to the point. They were fast-moving, slapstick chases around town with as many funny faces and gags as possible crammed into each reel. At first, Charlie was unsure of himself in the organisation. He had to learn film techniques and a less sophisticated form of comedy than he had been used to onstage. The studio often used local events as a backdrop and it was in 1914, in *Kid's Auto Races*, that Charlie's tramp character first made an appearance as a man in the crowd who continually gets in the way of the camera. As Charlie gained confidence in himself and his character, he began directing films. Sydney left England to join him but Charlie was soon hired by another film company, Essanay, on a much larger salary. His popularity soared, both in America and Europe, and he was nicknamed Charlot in France. He formed a music company with Sydney in 1916 and signed with another company, the Mutual Film

Corporation, for the astronomical sum of ten thousand dollars a week and a bonus of $150,000.

But war in Europe led some people to criticise Charlie for not fighting for his country. While he protested he was ready to be called up, others pointed out he was doing more for the soldiers in the trenches by making them laugh at his antics on screen. An element of sentimentality was creeping into his work. This only served to heighten his popularity as people identified with the little tramp and his battles with bullies and authority. Charlie's character had become Everyman.

Sydney was now managing Charlie's business affairs and the comedian's life style was becoming more luxurious, although he would always be careful with money. In 1917, Chaplin signed a lucrative contract with First National Exhibitors' Circuit which gave him even greater control over the production of his films. *A Dog's Life* (1918) was one of his best films, paralleling the life of a homeless mongrel dog with that of the tramp. Acute observation and irony plus a good storyline were the hallmarks of Chaplin films. He drove himself and his production team, working long hours in the days before union regulations. Such was his box office appeal that he joined his friend Douglas Fairbanks and Fairbanks's sweetheart, Mary Pickford, in touring the country to encourage the sale of bonds to help the American war effort.

Charlie was now Hollywood's most eligible bachelor, with his pick of glamorous women. At a party thrown by Samuel Goldwyn, he met a sixteen year-old actress, Mildred Harris. She looked young for her age; they began an affair. When Mildred told Charlie she was pregnant, he felt obliged to do the right thing and marry the girl in September 1918. But he was soon bored with Mildred and she was unhappy with his commitment to his work. Soon after the wedding, Mildred announced she wasn't pregnant, after all, and Charlie felt trapped in a loveless marriage. He believed the enforced domesticity was draining his creativity as he struggled with his work at the studio.

When Mildred gave birth in July 1919 to a sickly son, who died three days later, Charlie sat down and cried. It was, perhaps, a cathartic breakdown. Now, with renewed energy, Charlie launched himself and the four year-old Jackie Coogan into the classic *The Kid*, one of his best remembered films. He was rarely at home and his marriage foundered. Mildred divorced him in 1920 but it would not be long before another young actress would command his attention. Lita Grey was only twelve years old when she first worked with Chaplin, in the dream sequence of *The Kid*, although it was to be another four years before Charlie would make her his bride, and not in circumstances of his choosing.

Meanwhile, learning that the big film companies were out to break the earning power of popular screen stars, he joined ranks with Douglas Fairbanks, Mary Pickford and D.W. Griffith in 1919 to create their own film company: United Artists. By 1921, a year after his divorce, Charlie felt confident enough to bring his mother to live in California. After all she had been through, Hannah's religion now had a strong hold on her and, on her arrival at immigration, she was convinced that one of the officials was Jesus Christ, himself. Charlie found her a home in South Hollywood where she would enjoy good health, as well as difficult periods of mental instability. But she was not fazed when her third son, whom she hadn't seen since his father had taken him from her at six months old, came to see her. She simply asked him to sit down and have a cup of tea with her. Young Wheeler Dryden was now working for his half-brother Charlie, as well as Sydney. Chaplin had assembled a regular team of actors and technicians around him and filming was now very much a family affair.

Rich and successful, Charlie was seized with nostalgia and a hankering to see the old country, as well as Paris and other capital cities. But he was unprepared for his reception in Europe. Everywhere he went, the police had difficulty in controlling the crowds who waited to greet him at ports and railway stations. In an interview with the press he mentioned his desire to visit Russia, a country he admired for its social reconstruction after the war and revolution. He wandered around his old haunts in Lambeth and saw the old familiar poverty with fresh eyes. He was feted by such luminaries as H.G. Wells and J.M. Barrie. Moving on to Berlin, he met the exotic Polish actress, Pola Negri, who would turn up again, in Hollywood, to haunt him. Nostalgia sated, he returned to California and his work, and began associating with intellectuals, in particular those who were enthusiastic about the new Communist Russia. In 1922, the newly-formed Federal Bureau of Investigation, the intelligence organisation run by J. Edgar Hoover, saw fit to open a file in the name of Charlie Chaplin.

Charlie was lonely and Pola Negri was in town. Soon, the actress was telling the press that she and Charlie were engaged to be married. It took a few months for the comedian to convince her that he was not the marrying kind. Yet, he built himself a luxury home next to Douglas Fairbanks, then set to work on *The Gold Rush*. For his leading lady, he chose Lita Grey: the girl who had caught his eye four years earlier. She was now fifteen and three-quarters. When Lita became pregnant in 1924, her mother and lawyer uncle left Charlie no choice but to marry in a hurry. If Lita's family had taken him to court, he could have been sent to prison for thirty years. But the shotgun wedding, in November 1924, left him angry and miserable, and he was impatient and critical of his young bride. Charlie Chaplin Junior was born in May 1925 but the birth was kept from the press for a while. Charlie went to New York where he conducted a passionate affair with the eighteen year-old Louise Brooks for two months. Lita became pregnant again and Sydney Chaplin Junior was born in March 1926, while Charlie was having an affair with Lita's friend, Merna Kennedy, now Charlie's new leading lady. By November that year, Lita had left the marital home with her two sons. Charlie hunkered down for an expensive divorce, protecting his work from the lawyers as best he could. While he was waiting for the court case, he was hit from another direction. The IRS sent him a bill for over a million dollars in unpaid taxes.

The divorce nearly broke Charlie emotionally and was intended to do the same financially. His hair turned white and he was obliged to dye it to continue filming. But his popularity on the screen remained and buoyed him up, as did the support of many intellectuals, particularly in France. He won a special Oscar in 1928 for *The Circus* but he was about to face his greatest challenge: the advent of sound in the movies. Charlie realised his tramp character would disappoint if he talked on film; he would no longer be a universal figure. In *City Lights*, he introduced sound to the story but steered clear of dialogue.

Hannah Chaplin died in August 1928 and Charlie was much affected by her death. He visited Europe again and talked politics with leading politicians, such as Lloyd George, and writers and thinkers, such as George Bernard Shaw and Gandhi. He saw the rise of the Nazi party when he visited Germany. Sydney was now living in Nice, in the South of France, for part of the year and Charlie enjoyed being a playboy on the French Riviera. He spent two months in Switzerland, in the mountain resort of St Moritz, with Sydney and Douglas Fairbanks. He and Sydney went on to Singapore, Bali and Tokyo. By the time Charlie returned to California, the Depression had hit America.

In his one and a half years away from Hollywood, Charlie noticed how much the world had changed and, in particular, how labour was being exploited. He had avoided the Wall Street Crash, himself, by turning his stock into cash; he was well-read when it came to economics. At a yacht party, he met Paulette Goddard, a newly-divorced actress who was full of life, and the couple hit it off immediately. Paulette also got on well with Charlie's two sons, who he had hardly seen since his divorce. Charlie bought a 38ft cruiser for his leisure time and began work on the script for his next film, *Modern Times*. His domestic life was happier than it had been for years. Paulette understood his commitment to his work. The couple sailed away to Honolulu and China in 1936 and returned, married. But Paulette was an ambitious actress and auditioned for the lead in *Gone with the Wind*.

While Charlie was working on his masterpiece *The Great Dictator*, in which he parodied Hitler and Mussolini, the couple began to drift apart. They divorced in Mexico in 1942 but remained on good terms. Later, Paulette would live in Switzerland and see Charlie from time to time.

But storm clouds were gathering around Charlie. His final speech in *The Great Dictator*, in which he spoke of humanity being annihilated by greed and violence, was embraced by the Communist Party in England and alarmed the right wing in America. The House of Un-American Activities Committee, the HUAC, had begun its investigations in 1939. Charlie's speeches in 1942, in favour of supporting Russia against the Nazis, as well as addressing his audiences as 'comrades', were duly noted. But another, more personal, situation was brewing. Her name was Joan Barry.

This time, when the phone rang, Lady Chaplin was there. Her daughter picked up the receiver, just as she had done on each occasion during the last ten weeks, and waited.

'You got the photo?' The heavily-accented voice was instantly recognisable after twenty or so calls, but the man had sounded less confident in the past couple of weeks, more eager to reach a deal.

'Yes, we did. It's my father's coffin, alright. Where have you taken him? Is the body still in - ?'

'You ask too many questions, as usual. All you have to do is pay us and we will tell you where your father is.'

'It's not that simple,' Geraldine shot a look at Superintendent Gabriel Cettou, who nodded his encouragement. 'It takes time to get so much money together. The bank is being difficult – '

'Don't play games with me!' the man spluttered angrily. 'We have been patient for too long! You have a little brother, *non*? We will shoot him on his way to school if you don't meet our terms immediately – '

'No, please, don't do that!' Geraldine was truly alarmed at the thought of young Christopher being attacked. 'My mother is already ill with the stress of this – '

'Then pay us now! The new price, the one we agreed. Quarter of a million Swiss francs in used notes. The railway station – '

'Look, give me a bit longer.' She glanced at Lady Chaplin, then at the policeman. 'I'll speak to my mother again. She can talk to the bank. Please give us another week. Please … ' The dialling tone sounded. The man had rung off.

'Huh, they won't get a dime of my money,' said her mother, finishing her drink. 'Your father would be outraged if he thought we'd given a centime to those crooks. The whole episode is as ridiculous as one of his Keystone capers: one hundred policemen, running from phone box to phone box, trying to trace a call – '

'We have established their movements, *Madame*,' explained Superintendent Cettou patiently. 'I can assure you these men will be arrested very soon.'

'They can go to hell, I say,' said Lady Chaplin, fixing herself another drink. 'A Keystone caper, that's what it is. Charlie never liked those one-reelers.'

Charlie's favourite way of keeping fit, as well as socialising, was a game of tennis. His weekly tennis parties were large, popular affairs where Hollywood came to be seen and mix with the best players of the day, such as Helen Wills and Fred Perry. Joan Barry, known variously as Joan Berry, Joanne Berry, Joan Barrett, Mary L. Barrett and Mary Louise Barry, in pursuit of a Hollywood career, was a guest at one of these parties in 1941 and soon began an affair with Chaplin. She was a mature woman by Charlie's standards: twenty-two years old, previously married and in the process of ending an affair with the millionaire J. Paul Getty, as long as Getty paid her to get out of his life. Joan wanted to be in the movies and Charlie was happy to pay for her to go to film school and give her a contract with his studio. By the following year, Joan had lost interest in acting but not in Charlie. Chaplin paid her off and terminated her contract, but Joan wouldn't remove herself from his life. She would phone continually or turn up, often drunk and hysterical, at his house during the night and smash windows. She even crashed the Cadillac J. Paul Getty had bought her in Charlie's driveway.

When Barry announced she was pregnant, Charlie arranged an abortion and paid off her debts and hoped that was the end of it. In October 1942, he was in New York, making speeches in support of the Russian war effort. Joan Barry came to his hotel and stayed the night. The affair dragged on. In December, Joan climbed a ladder and broke into Charlie's home. She was toting a gun. She stayed the night again and Charlie gave her some money. A week later, she returned. This time, Chaplin called the police. Barry was given a suspended sentence and ordered to leave town. In May 1943, Joan Barry was given thirty days for vagrancy, most of which she spent in hospital. She was six months pregnant.

Meanwhile, Charlie had met Oona, the beautiful seventeen year-old daughter of the playwright, Eugene O'Neill. Oona moved into Charlie's home and they decided to marry as soon as she was eighteen. The gossip columnists were having a field day: Hedda Hopper was particularly vitriolic in her articles on Charlie, while the FBI was trailing Chaplin, convinced he was a Communist. Joan Barry filed a paternity suit against Charlie, who denied he was the father of her child. He was obliged to support her and the unborn child until a blood test could decide the case, once and for all, or so Charlie imagined. Oona and Charlie married in June 1943, much to the disapproval of her father, who disowned her. In October that year, Joan Barry gave birth to a girl. The FBI were following the case closely. They not only interviewed Joan, repeatedly, but Charlie's sons, his staff and even Oona, who knew nothing about Barry. In 1944, Charlie was fingerprinted in front of the press, tried and found not guilty of fathering Joan's child; the blood test proved it. But the FBI had the ear of the judge and a retrial was ordered on a technical detail.

In August that year, Geraldine, Charlie and Oona's first child was born. Charlie was confident the second paternity suit would go his way but the prosecution hammered away at his morals and character and he reacted badly to the lawyers in the courtroom. In the end, the jury could not decide if Charlie had committed a crime or not. Another retrial, another jury. The blood tests were ignored, as they could be in Californian law at that time, and Chaplin was found guilty. He was obliged to support the baby girl until she was twenty-one. Joan Barry married again and had two more children before she was committed to hospital in a confused state. Charlie was deeply hurt by the damage the case had done to his reputation and he turned to Oona and his new family for consolation.

Oona worshipped Charlie and her love and support enabled him to return to work. But his next film, *Monsieur Verdoux*, was panned and, at the press conference afterwards, journalists seemed more intent on quizzing him about his Communist sympathies. The House of Un-American Activities Committee summoned him to appear before them in 1947. It was viewed with suspicion that Charlie had never felt patriotic enough to become a United States citizen. Charlie realised that if he tried to visit England with his family, his re-entry permit would probably be cancelled. With the FBI sifting for evidence of wrong-doing and the news that he would be obliged to lodge a bond of one and a half million dollars if he left the country, Charlie postponed any trips abroad and focussed on the last of his great films, *Limelight*.

His film company, United Artists, was now a million dollars in debt. It took a lot of legal wrangling to agree on a financial solution with his business partner, Mary Pickford. *Limelight* was in part an autobiographical film, based on Charlie's parents and his music hall days. His children were given parts and the actress Claire Bloom was brought from England to play the leading lady. Even Oona was involved in the film-making. The film served to intensify Charlie's homesickness. Those last few years in America had disillusioned him and he longed for Europe again. In 1952, he made the decision to hold the world première of *Limelight* in London. He knew what this meant. In September 1952, the Chaplin family sailed from

New York to Southampton. Two days out, at sea, Charlie was informed he was barred from re-entering the States. The FBI soon renewed the permit, with the caveat that it was no guarantee he could re-enter the country. But Charlie had already made his plans.

The busy centre of Lausanne: a bright May morning in 1978. Two long-haired men in leather jackets crammed in a phone box, holding a receiver between them, listening to a call. Some way off, a police siren wails, getting closer. A tall, fit-looking man, neatly-dressed and standing nearby, peers over the top of his newspaper towards the phone kiosk, as if waiting for the men to finish their call. Does he glance at someone studying a bus stop timetable on the other side of the Place St François? Does he also look over his shoulder at two men with shopping bags on the opposite pavement, talking casually and smoking cigarettes?

    The men in the phone box seem to be having a disagreement. One has snatched the phone from the other. The taller one grabs it back. They are pulling the receiver one way then the other and arguing in some East European tongue. They are still wrestling with the phone as the neatly-dressed man opens the kiosk door. Perhaps he needs to make a call urgently and is growing tired of the two men jostling in the kiosk. Perhaps he is acting in some kind of official capacity; he is waving some sort of ID at them, just as a Swiss policeman might do when making an arrest. Now, he has his hand on the shoulder of one of the long-haired men. He is replacing the receiver for him. The two men with shopping bags have jettisoned their cigarettes and bags and joined him, so has the man who was studying the bus timetable across the way. Handcuffs have appeared, sirens are ear-splittingly close now. Shoppers have stopped to watch the scene. The two men are yanked from the call box and bundled into the back of a police car. The episode has created quite a diversion in the street. Not something Swiss shoppers are used to.

Charlie was bombarded with questions by the press when he and his family docked at Southampton in September 1952. Would he return to the United States after his trip? What were his politics? Would he face any charges brought against him by the American government? The couple remained vague about their plans and said how much Charlie was looking forward to showing London to Oona. The family wealth was still in America. Charlie could not afford to rock the White House boat. But there were many people, on both sides of the Atlantic, who felt the world's greatest comedian had been treated unfairly, and were courageous enough to speak out against McCarthyism and the HUAC's hounding of artists and thinkers. The writer Graham Greene, who had become a friend, wrote an open letter to Charlie in the *New Statesman*, condemning the anti-Communist witch-hunt against him. The result was that Greene had his own problems obtaining a visa to enter the United States. The actor and playwright, Peter Ustinov, a future neighbour in Switzerland, made a BBC recording, strongly criticising the political paranoia in the States, and was asked to keep a low profile after it was broadcast. Georges Simenon, who had moved to the States, abandoned any plan to become an American citizen and began to think of returning to Europe.

Charlie, now sixty-three years old, insisted he was not a political man, simply an individualist who believed in liberty. His films were intended to amuse people, not create a revolution. The London première of *Limelight*, in October 1952, was a great success and attended by Princess Margaret. In Paris, Charlie was made an officer of the Légion d'Honneur and a member of the Société des Auteurs et Compositeurs Dramatiques, but the American Ambassador did not attend the première of the film. Back in the States, the columnist, Hedda Hopper, attacked Charlie, as well as Peter Ustinov. The American Legion did their best to disrupt performances of *Limelight* and it was withdrawn from picture houses.

In November, Oona Chaplin returned, quietly and alone, to New York. She went quickly to Hollywood, wound up Charlie's business affairs in the United States as best she could, and was back on a plane to Europe two days later. Charlie had been beside himself with worry that Oona would be stopped at immigration. They had never been apart before and it was not just his fortune that concerned him.

By December, 1952, Charlie and Oona Chaplin were in Switzerland and, like other international exiles, such as Coco Chanel, they took refuge in the Beau-Rivage Palace Hotel in Lausanne while they tried to sort out their lives. They soon found a home they loved: a palatial, colonnaded manor house with spectacular views over Lake Geneva and the Alps beyond, the Manoir de Ban at Corsier-sur-Vevey. They rented the property at first, ironically from a former American Ambassador. In February, they bought the house and Charlie looked forward to some peace and quiet. That was when he became aware of the rifle range at the edge of his thirty-seven acre parkland.

It is the right of every Swiss man to maintain the shooting skills he learned in the national army. Rifle stands abound in Switzerland and citizens practise regularly at their local range, even on Sunday mornings. The Swiss right to bear arms was established in the mists of time and is bound up with the myth of William Tell and his marksmanship with a crossbow and apple. The Commune of Vevey was understandably puzzled when they received Charlie's complaints. They were obliged by law to provide a firing range, like any other commune. But they were proud to have the great comedian as a resident and did everything they could to help with the problem. They limited practice times and put up a sound-proof barrier, but Charlie's complaints rumbled on. When the motorway that linked Montreux with Geneva arrived, Charlie threatened to decamp to the French Riviera where Sydney lived for part of the year with his second wife, Henrietta, known as Gypsy. Georges Simenon was also disturbed by the increasing road traffic and moved house in Lausanne.

The Chaplin family lived a basically American way of life in their fifteen-room villa, although Charlie insisted on an English breakfast before he disappeared into the library to work every day. He poured his still abundant energy into film scripts and, later, his autobiography. He hired a secretarial team, as well as around a dozen domestic servants, mostly Italian. Staff costs were one of Charlie's *bêtes-noires* and it was one of his secretaries who would be at the receiving end of his obsession with keeping down wages. The highly-qualified woman had taken a low-paid job with Charlie because she admired the man and his work. Charlie was an emotional boss with a tendency to act out every line he dictated. He would often fly into a rage if his work or business affairs were not going his way. After about a year of Charlie's tantrums, the secretary was in a state of nervous collapse. When Charlie fumed about the cost of his swimming pool construction and accused the secretary of being in cahoots with the contractors, at the very moment when the woman was on the phone to them, trying to sort out the problem, she resigned and fled the Manoir de Ban without collecting her wages. Later, the secretary would take Charlie to court for three month's back pay and holiday entitlement money. Charlie was obliged to pay up, but his last big financial battle would be with the U.S. tax authorities.

Charlie had gone to Geneva to hand in his American re-entry permit and Oona had renounced her American citizenship. As a 'non-resident alien', the U.S. Treasury calculated Charlie owed just over half a million dollars in back taxes in 1953. He refused to pay. The Treasury doubled the amount for overdue payment and added the following year's taxes, bringing the figure owed to nearly one and a half million. Still, Charlie refused to pay. His lawyers locked horns with the IRS and, over the next three years, the amount was whittled down to something like the original half a million. It would not be until 1972 that Charlie and Oona would return to New York and Hollywood, when a new generation, the baby-boomers who questioned authority, war and the exploitation of workers and race, would welcome the ageing comedian back and present him with another Oscar.

In October 1974, Charlie, now in a wheelchair, was knighted by Queen Elizabeth II at Buckingham Palace. Sir Charles Spencer Chaplin had come a long way since his vagabond days on the streets in Lambeth. He had worked on two more films since leaving Hollywood, neither of which were a great success, but his autobiography sold well in 1964 and captured the hearts of millions of readers as he recounted his childhood poverty and workhouse experiences. The book was well-written, but by whom? Chaplin laboured over the manuscript and dictated it several times over. Truman Capote, a neighbour in Switzerland, asked him how the work was progressing. Charlie thrust the manuscript in his hand and asked him to take it away and read it. When Capote returned it, having gone through it with a pencil to iron out what he saw as major faults and errors, Chaplin shouted that he had only meant Truman to read and enjoy the work. They never spoke again.

Ian Fleming, the urbane author of the James Bond novels, was staying in nearby Montreux with Charlie's good friend, Noël Coward, when they had dinner with the Chaplins at the Manoir de Ban. Fleming had the impression Charlie was on the home stretch with his memoir and tried to secure its serialisation for *The Sunday Times*. Georges Simenon was asked if he had assisted Charlie in writing the autobiography. Simenon said he hadn't but he knew an author who had. Graham Greene had been a guest at the manor house and had read Charlie's manuscript. How much input Greene was responsible for was never discussed by either man.

Charlie's brother, who had been a frequent visitor to Corsier, died in 1965 and is buried in Clarens Cemetery in Montreux, just a few graves away from the Russian writer, Vladimir Nabokov, another Montreux resident. Syd, who, unlike Charlie, had never lost his Lambeth cockney accent, was a popular uncle with Charlie's children. He would tell them ribald jokes and get them to repeat them to their father, much to Charlie's mortification. Charlie's relationship with his children was a distant one and, later on, difficult. His two sons by Lita Grey had found him testy and over-critical; he would often belittle them in front of others. His eldest, Charles Junior, was a sensitive soul who found solace in alcohol, like his grandfather. He died, not much older than Charlie's father, at the age of forty-three, from a fall and the neglect of his injury.

The Chaplin children at the Manoir de Ban called their father 'Fat Cheeks'. He was strict with them, often reminding them of his poverty in childhood, especially when they opened their presents on Christmas morning. Oona and Charlie were so wrapped up in their own relationship that they seemed to have little time for their children, who were brought up mainly by nannies. Geraldine left home to go to ballet school in London. Her rebellious brother, Michael, soon followed her and threw himself into the Swinging Sixties, marriage and a period on the dole. Victoria eloped with a French actor and later married him. Oona was obliged to speak to the press about her eldest son, but she kept a weather eye on her children from afar. As Charlie lost his fire and energy and slipped into old age, the family were all reconciled.

Charlie had been a popular figure in the nearby town of Vevey. He would attend showings of his films and take his children to the circus that regularly came to town.

He stopped travelling and remained at home, going only as far as the lake by car with Oona and sitting there for an hour or so before returning to the Manoir. He suffered suspected strokes and insisted that Oona, alone, nurse him. She exhausted herself catering to his every need. She damaged her back, carrying him to the toilet. But she was devoted to him. The man had been her whole life. On Christmas morning in 1977, Charlie Chaplin passed away in his sleep. Two days later, he was buried in the local cemetery at Corsier-sur-Vevey with the British Ambassador present. On 1 March 1978, Charlie rose again, or someone helped him out of his grave.

When the grave robbers contacted the family, Oona would have nothing to do with their demands. She didn't care where her husband was, she declared; he was in her heart and in heaven, and that was enough. But her children worked with the police, who patiently closed their net on the robbers. It took twenty-seven phone calls, with Geraldine Chaplin in the role of a bereaved and concerned daughter, to track the criminals down. The two were finally caught making a call from a kiosk in Lausanne and were brought to trial the following December. Roman Wardas, a twenty-four year-old Polish unemployed car mechanic, was the 'brains' behind the operation. With his sidekick, thirty-eight year-old Gantcho Ganev, a Bulgarian garage mechanic working in Lausanne, they had tried to copy the kidnapping of the body of an Italian industrialist and use the money to set themselves up in a car repairs business. Wardas was given a four and a half years' sentence for disturbing the dead and extortion. Ganev was handed a suspended sentence of one and a half years. They had buried Charlie's body in a cornfield where

Wardas used to go fishing, just outside the village of Noville, near Montreux, at the end of the lake. Oona declared the spot so calm when she saw it that she thought it was, in some ways, more peaceful than the site in the cemetery. The farmer who owned the field erected a wooden cross in Charlie's memory and decorated it with a cane. Someone laid flowers there for many years afterwards. Oona tried to fill her days, but her world had collapsed.

Like her father, Eugene O'Neill, Oona liked a drink. When Charlie had been difficult or demanding, she would take a glass or two and retire. Oona had been obliged to leave her homeland and live in Europe, a continent she had never visited before she lived there. Now she spent as much time as her tax situation would allow back in the States and spent money on refurbishing the Manoir de Ban and buying pictures. But the knowledge that Charlie would not approve of so much expenditure took all the pleasure out of these shopping sprees.

In her final years, Oona would sit in her room, playing videos, time and again, believing she was watching them for the first time. Her health deteriorated; she couldn't keep down her food. The children did all they could to support their mother throughout the 1980's but, finally, in August 1991, Oona Chaplin was diagnosed with cancer of the pancreas. She died, aged sixty-six, the following month and was buried alongside Charlie. At her request, her coffin was encased in concrete, as her husband's had been on its return to the grave site. They lie only a few headstones away from their old friend, the actor James Mason.

Across the road, on the other side of the route that leads from Vevey to Charlie Chaplin Park, Charlie's supporter in troubled times, the writer Graham Greene, was laid to rest in April 1991, just a few months before Oona. Like Charlie, Greene had loved, and been loved by, many women and had his share of troubles with the tax authorities. But his journey to the Swiss Riviera had taken a very different path, in a life as dramatic and eventful as any of his novels or plays.

Chapter 3
Graham Greene

'**A** licence to print money, gentleman! That's how I see our little enterprise!' George Sanders, suave Hollywood actor, leaned back in his capacious leather chair and regarded the two stout men across the table. 'Thomas, as an international lawyer specialising in tax avoidance, we rely on you to persuade the rich and famous on the Swiss Riviera to invest in our new company.' Tom Roe nodded happily and adjusted his thick-framed glasses. 'I, myself, will convince my motion picture chums that we've created an opportunity not to be missed. Dennis ... ' Sanders threw Loraine, the small-time fraudster, one of his famous supercilious looks, 'I believe your – ah – Royal Victoria Sausages Limited has the right product to attract the punters.'

'Like I said, mate,' Loraine gesticulated enthusiastically. 'It's the bleedin' recipe. Found it on a bit o' paper in the old butcher's shop I bought, down in Brighton. Had the date on it: 1919. Straight up.' His chubby hand slapped the polished table top. 'Secret recipe, it said, for the favourite sausages of none other than King Edward VII!'

'Yes, well,' drawled Sanders, glancing at Tom Roe. 'I think we'll keep that secret to ourselves, Dennis, if you don't mind. If I remember correctly, the venerable Edward VII died in 1910. Now then, Thomas, who are our latest investors? Charlie Chaplin contacted me after he spoke with you. He's in for a good amount. James Hadley Chase, likewise, and Noël Coward, I'm delighted to say. I've spoken to Bill Holden and he's happy to be on board. Likewise, Bob Mitchum in L.A. – '

'I've been thinking, George – '

'Don't, Dennis. It doesn't become you.'

'What we need – I mean, really need, for seeing top people, like, is a jet!'

'Good heavens ... '

'Straight up. A company jet! Looks good. Like your new Roller and Tom's château – '

'I've told you,' said Roe, his round face clouding for a moment, 'it's not a château. They're called villas, here in Lausanne. A large one, I admit – '

'And you can afford it, Thomas, now Graham Greene is fully committed to our project! Did I understand correctly, Greene has invested every penny he has in our little scheme?'

"Ere! Is that the writer? *The Third Man*, and that stuff?'

'As opposed to the plumber, Dennis.'

Roe readjusted his glasses and was beaming again. 'Graham didn't take much persuading. Loves sausages. Hates tax. Our biggest investor, to date. Worth hundreds of thousands!'

'Then, Dennis, as a token of our thanks for your, ah, secret recipe, you may look at private aeroplanes with a view to purchasing one. Nothing vulgar, mind ... '

Graham Greene, one of the great writers of the twentieth century, was born in the market town of Berkhamsted in Hertfordshire, to the north-west of London, on 2 October 1904. He was the fourth of six children born to Charles Greene, headmaster of the local public school, St. John's, and his wife Marion. The couple were devoted to each other but seemed remote to their children, who were consigned to the nursery and the care of a nanny; normal practice in upper middle-class families in Edwardian England before the Great War.

The Greenes were well-connected on both sides of the family: Marion Greene was first cousin to the writer Robert Louis Stevenson and her husband, Charles, was related to the wealthy Greene brewing family of Bury St Edmunds. There were two distinct branches of Greenes in the Berkhamsted area. Charles's family of academics, who lived on the school premises, surrounded by books, was less moneyed than his brother Edward's brood, who, in spite of their wealth from Brazilian coffee, regarded their intellectual cousins with awe. But the families were close and spent Christmases together, playing charades and word games. Later, as a young adult, Henry Graham Greene, as Graham had been christened, would travel and share adventures with his cousins that would shape his character and attitude, and bring a perceptiveness to his writing that would be known as Greeneland.

The intellectual Greenes were achievers. Raymond, the first-born son, was an excellent sportsman and explorer and became a top London surgeon. Youngest brother, Hugh, would become Director General of the BBC, while baby sister, Elisabeth, the last-born, would introduce Graham to the world of espionage and the British Intelligence Service. Only the second son, Herbert, would disappoint and constantly cause anxiety to his parents as he flitted around the world, getting fired from one job after another. In later years, Graham would be exasperated by Herbert's escapades and abortive money-making schemes. But, in his childhood and youth, Graham Greene was mostly frustrated with himself.

A deeply sensitive child, frightened of the dark and unable to sleep without his large collection of soft toy animals in bed every night, Graham played happily with his younger siblings in the nursery where he was given private lessons until he was eight. A green baize door separated the family's living quarters from the very different environment of St John's school, with its noises, smells, rules and disciplined way of life. The door became a symbolic frontier post, beyond which, it seemed to Graham, lay a hostile world of strict school masters, teasing boys and dreaded sports lessons. At preparatory school, he was shy, gauche and spoke with a slight lisp and, although he made an effort to get along with other pupils, he was happiest in the school holidays when he could lose himself in books in the school library, particularly the adventure stories of his near-relative Robert Louis Stevenson, as well as Rider Haggard and John Buchan. These tales were to give Greene his yearning for travel and incident and would lead to his admiration of the novels of Joseph Conrad, particularly *Heart of Darkness*. He would remain restless and romantic about exploring new countries to the end of his days.

It was when he entered St John's senior school that life became difficult for Graham. His father was the headmaster and, no matter how Greene tried to fit in, he felt his fellow pupils were suspicious of him, as they would be of a spy in their midst. His older brothers did not appear to have had this sense of being an outsider, with loyalties divided between home and school. Perhaps Graham was simply more sensitive than Raymond and Herbert had been. Nevertheless, children are quick to sense fragility in another and, by the time he was fourteen, Graham had become the victim of a subtle bully called Carter; an experience that would mark him for the rest of his life and influence his story-telling.

Carter knew just how to torment Graham, how to offer just enough hope of friendship, then snatch it away. In class, he would prod the hapless Greene with a pair of compass dividers or pounce on Greene's personal diary and read it out loud to the other boys. But the cruellest blow of all was delivered by a boy named Wheeler, who Graham believed to be a friend. Having confided in Wheeler, the jubilant boy promptly sided with Carter against him. Greene never forgot the betrayal and the theme of disloyalty was to feature repeatedly in his writing.

Graham suffered in silence. He could not share his problems with his father, for that would have been seen as siding with authority. And he could not, as a boarder, retreat into the solitude he needed to deal with the situation. Instead, he turned his anxiety inwards, and there followed a series of attempts at self-harm. On one occasion, he tried to saw open his knee with a penknife. On another, he swallowed an amount of fixing fluid in the photography dark room; another time, the contents of a bottle of hay-fever drops. He ate deadly nightshade on the local common, which left him feeling a little high. He tried swallowing a number of aspirins and throwing himself into the school swimming baths. Finally, at the end of the long summer holiday, when he felt he couldn't bear another school year with Carter and Wheeler, he ran away from home, leaving a note for his parents saying he would never return unless he could be excused school. His elder sister found him hiding in the bushes on the common. His parents were deeply concerned. When they understood the torment their son had been going through, Carter was removed from the school. But the bully-boy tactics had already taken effect: Graham developed a persecution complex and suffered a nervous breakdown. From then on, his sympathies would lie with the underdog, the hunted individual. He now knew enough about divided loyalty, persecution and betrayal to create unbearable tensions for the characters in his novels over decades to come.

It was his eldest brother, Raymond, now a medical student, who recommended the psychiatrist Kenneth Richmond to his parents as someone who could help Graham through his crisis. Richmond had successfully treated other schoolboys, with the added bonus that he had literary connections. Based in London, the unconventional Richmond and his spiritualist wife believed in guiding patients to self-healing, particularly through the analysis of dreams, and their house in Devonshire Terrace was, for the sixteen year-old Graham, a new and exciting world, far removed from school life in Berkhamsted.

The complete change of environment seemed to help Greene, and his stay with the Richmonds in 1921 gave him ample free time to discover London. He visited museums and galleries and enjoyed the cinema and theatre, where he was deeply aroused by one particular actress. He was now strongly attracted to the opposite sex and would observe, but never dare to speak to, the young nannies pushing their prams in Kensington Gardens. When one of his girl cousins, Ave, joined him on Richmond's course, they would slip into the Old Bailey court house in the afternoons and watch the most interesting cases from the public gallery.

Graham was already writing down his observations and had been paid a modest amount for a sketch he had sent to a London paper. He was delighted when the Richmonds introduced him to writers and editors they knew, and bowled over when one of his favourite poets, Walter de la Mare, came to tea. Graham returned to Berkhamsted for his last few terms of school a different young man. He had been stimulated by the sophisticated world of literary London and had gained a new self-confidence, as well as a contempt for rules and tradition. He was still an outsider at Berkhamsted but less timid now and sometimes a prankster in lessons. He found his voice in school debates and wrote for the school magazine. He wrote a play and sent it off to London where it was accepted by a drama group, but never staged. In 1922, he finally escaped Berkhamsted altogether for Balliol College, Oxford, where he chose to study Modern History.

At Balliol, he joined like-minded students in playing jokes and testing authority. On one occasion the young men dressed as tramps and toured the countryside with a barrel organ. Japes like this provided some relief from boredom; alcohol was another stimulant. Greene reckoned he was hardly ever sober at university, but he could handle his drink well. He was a more sociable person now and had begun to make literary contacts and write articles for the press. But he avoided tutorials in favour of reading alone in his rooms. His history degree took second place while he focussed on new ideas and his plans for the future.

Graham had enjoyed the barrel organ episode, the dressing-up and assuming another identity. It harked back to the spy stories he had read as a boy and he knew he could turn such incidents into articles, which meant he would be paid for having a grand adventure. A trip to Ireland in 1923 was funded by the *Weekly Westminster Gazette* in return for his impressions of Dublin and Republican feeling at the time. In 1924, he approached the German Embassy, proposing a fact-finding tour of the Ruhr with two other undergraduates to report on how the local population was being treated under French occupation after World War I. This prompted a visit from an intelligence officer at the embassy, a certain Count von Bernstorff, who travelled to Oxford to check out Greene before handing him a generous amount of money to fund the students' trip. During their fortnight on the Rhine and the Moselle, searching for incidents and stories, Graham could sense German hostility to all foreigners, particularly the French. The students decided to turn their travels into a Buchan-style thriller novel, but it was Graham who was already thinking of becoming a professional spy. Count von Bernstorff continued to meet with him but the situation in the Ruhr resolved itself and Graham found other 'ways of escape' from boredom, as he would later describe his activities and travels. The mysterious Count was later to be executed by the Nazis in the Second World War when he was caught helping Jews escape to Switzerland.

Graham now plunged himself into literary activities at university, making useful contacts in the publishing world. He was one of a group of students who read their poetry on BBC radio and became President of the Modern Poetry and Drama Society. He acted as editor of the *Oxford Outlook* magazine and changed its publisher in an attempt to get the publication to pay its way. He was now very attracted to the opposite sex and, after glimpsing the bare leg of the family nanny on a beach during the summer holiday in 1924, he promptly fell in love with her. The woman was ten years older than he was and engaged to be married, but he still pleaded with her to break with her fiancé. The nanny married in 1925 and Greene's passion ran its course, but he had taken to playing Russian roulette with his brother's revolver on

Berkhamsted Common in the holidays. He had read a book by a Russian writer who described White Russian officers using live ammunition in a bid to escape boredom. This appealed to Greene and he would experiment half a dozen times with Raymond's gun, partly because he was, himself, bored and partly to test his courage, which had failed him at school when he'd been bullied by Carter.

Graham became a manic depressive: his moods would swing from extreme highs to appalling lows. He was hyperactive, throwing himself into countless activities to ward off the depression that threatened to engulf him. He and another student joined the Communist Party for four weeks in the autumn of 1924. Their aim was to secure funding for a trip to Paris and to write an article based on their visit to the Communist headquarters there. They were invited to attend a workers' meeting but they soon lost interest and slipped out to roam the streets, gawking at prostitutes but not daring to approach them. In Sylvia Beach's bookshop, Graham bought a copy of James Joyce's *Ulysses*, which had been banned in England. His own style of writing at this time was romantic, rather than modernist, and he would later try to buy up all the sold copies of his volume of poetry and prose, *Babbling April*, which had been published by Blackwell's, the Oxford publisher, in 1923.

It was through Blackwell's that Greene met his future wife, Vivien, in 1925. She was a secretary at the publishers and Graham, in his last year at university, was looking for a job that would develop into a career. He had already been turned down by the Asiatic Petroleum Company, since they doubted that writers made good company employees. *The Times* newspaper told him to go off and get some journalistic experience on a provincial paper. An article he had written in the *Oxford Outlook* prompted a letter of criticism from Vivien. Graham invited her to tea to discuss the article and fell madly in love with her.

Vivien was a pretty girl and had several admirers. She was also a Catholic, whereas Greene was an atheist. But Graham pursued her and bombarded her with hundreds of love letters, often several a day. Vivien had also published a book of verse and appreciated Greene's writing talent and, gradually, fell in love with him. But they could not marry until Graham had a regular job. He had turned down a three-year stint in China with the British American Tobacco Company, partly because he found his fellow employees excruciatingly dull and partly to remain near Vivien. He took a temporary job as a private tutor to a ten year-old boy in Derbyshire, but the job brought him close to another nervous breakdown. He had, early on, formed the habit of writing five hundred words every day, but the two novels he'd written had already been rejected. He despaired of ever finding work that he enjoyed and fell into another depression. Then his old tutor at Balliol, Kenneth Bell, offered to help him find a job on a provincial newspaper. Greene had been producing articles on a freelance basis. Now, he approached a number of papers in the north of England and landed a post as a sub-editor on *The Nottingham Journal*. This would give him the experience he needed in journalism and provide a stepping stone to the London papers.

During his four months in the provinces, Greene shook off his depression. The team of editorial staff were welcoming and he was soon enthusiastic about his work and good at his job. The working-class town and his seedy digs would provide him with material for *A Gun for Sale* (1936) and while he was living there, with marriage in mind, he converted to Catholicism. He also indulged his love of films and spent many hours in the cheap matinée seats of the local cinemas. He liked to view movies alone and the mood of a film would often spark creative thoughts for his writing. But Graham realised there was no future for him in Nottingham and he packed his bag and headed for London. Having failed to find a post on any of the capital's papers, he became depressed, once more, and talked of ending his engagement to Vivien. Then, in March 1926, he finally landed a job as a sub-editor on *The Times*. His hours were four in the afternoon until eleven at night: plenty of time to write novels during the day, as well as book reviews for other papers.

Graham was a hard worker and efficient at his job. He liked his colleagues and soon relaxed into a calm and happy state. A couple of months after he joined the paper, the General Strike brought a welcome new excitement into his life. *The Times* continued to print every day and Greene enjoyed doing the work of the striking packers, as well as his own job. He had not yet come to appreciate the plight of union members, how oppressed and poor they were. He could only see the episode as an adventure and hoped the conflict would continue and become violent. He was also made a special constable, but he soon became bored with patrolling Vauxhall Bridge. It was not until the Great Depression of the 1930's that Graham would come to sympathise with the workers.

All the time he was hoping to become a successful novelist, continuing to write those five hundred words every morning, even when he would rather not. He worried that the effort it took him meant he was not truly a writer, unlike his cousin, Christopher Isherwood. But he had not yet found his authorial voice; he was still trying to imitate writers he admired, like Joseph Conrad. When his second book was rejected, he made up his mind to write one last novel before giving up on fiction altogether and, perhaps, turning to film script writing.

The date and place was set for Graham and Vivien's wedding: 15 October 1927 in Hampstead, where the couple had found a small flat. Graham was driving himself harder than ever, trying to earn as much money as possible from his writing. Even when he collapsed at work with appendicitis, he continued turning out book reviews in hospital, fearing he would be replaced by another reviewer. During his stay in hospital, he never ceased to observe what was going on around him. With the alertness and curiosity of a writer, he was the only patient on his ward not to turn away and retreat into his radio headphones when an old man passed away from cancer, followed by a young boy with a broken leg who died after his operation. Graham listened with interest to the wailing grief of the boy's mother at the bedside, realising that a writer needed a certain cold objectivity in order to gather material.

His convalescence in Brighton, where he had enjoyed family holidays as a child, was to provide the location and colourful characters for one of his most famous novels, *Brighton Rock*. An eccentric old man he had met one evening in a shelter on the seafront was transformed into the luckless Hale, who would be found dead in a similar shelter, a piece of Brighton rock candy, it is implied, forced down his throat. Brighton's Kemptown races and the razor gangs who haunted them, as well as the assizes in the nearby county town of Lewes, would also provide dramatic scenes for the novel. Wherever he went, Greene absorbed details of his surroundings. As a writer, he was always on duty. On his first day back at work at *The Times* after his illness, he fainted. He began to daydream of travelling as a way of escaping the treadmill he felt he was on. Berlin was in contact again. Spying seemed a wonderful way to earn extra money.

When under stress, Graham would have a night on the town with a friend. He would anaesthetise himself with drink and divert himself with prostitutes, a pattern that would continue throughout his relationship with his wife and his love affairs, later on. Greene was very much in love with Vivien at first, and she was continually supportive and a great source of stability when his novels were rejected. His passion for the cinema led him to review films for *The Times*. As always, Graham was alert to details and techniques he could use in his writing. Finally, in March 1928, after working for two years on another novel, as well as sub-editing at *The Times* and producing book and film reviews, Heinemann accepted his manuscript of *The Man Within* for publication and the novel was a great success both in Europe and in America.

Graham now plunged into the social side of literary success, meeting authors he admired, such as the commercial writer, Edgar Wallace, and the classic novelist, Arnold Bennett. But success gave him an unrealistic confidence in his ability to produce best-sellers. Greene decided to become a full-time writer and gave in his notice at *The Times*. His colleagues and the editor tried to dissuade him; Graham was well-liked and excellent at his job. But Greene had exhausted himself by holding down several occupations. He longed for time to himself to think and write his next book. He left *The Times* at the end of 1929, only months after the Wall Street Crash. The black clouds of the Great Depression were beginning to gather.

For the next fourteen months, Greene would struggle to produce another best-seller. Reviews of his next two books were not complimentary and sales were limited. He wrote short stories to bring in some much needed cash, and all the time he was journeying restlessly: to Woodstock in Oxford and Hardy's birthplace in the West Country, to Oberammergau in Bavaria and Constantinople, which would later feature in *Stamboul Train*, and a cruise in the Aegean. But time and money ran out, and Greene and Vivien were obliged to sub-let their flat in Hampstead in March 1931 and move to a simple cottage in Chipping Campden, in the Cotswolds. Graham hated the isolation and took to striding out on long walks across the countryside, as well as trips to London where he mixed business with pleasure.

As another diversion, he began work on a biography of the licentious John Wilmot, second Earl of Rochester, but it would be another forty-three years before Greene's account of the rake's life was considered acceptable for publication. Now desperately short of money, depressed and in debt, he hit on the idea of writing 'an entertainment', as he would later classify his stories he considered less serious than others. Based on a train journey of several characters on the Orient Express, *Stamboul Train* had all the elements that took Greene out of himself: travel, the acute observation of others, tense situations and a dramatic finish.

Greene was now so short of money that he could only research part of the train route by travelling second class as far as Cologne. But it was enough to give him the details and atmosphere he needed to write a commercial thriller. Even at this stage he was thinking of film rights and his style became taut and realistic, his descriptions like a camera shot evoking a certain mood. It was his last throw of the dice: he was flat broke and thinking of taking a teaching post abroad. Nevertheless, he believed that *Stamboul Train* was good in parts and, when he'd finished it, he headed for London to lose himself in the bright lights and gaudy women.

With an income tax demand he couldn't pay hanging over his head, Graham waited for the publisher's opinion of his novel. He was not only depressed but at screaming point, literally, with those around him. Less than two weeks after he had posted the manuscript to Heinemann he couldn't help writing to them, asking them for their verdict. To his great joy and relief the book was accepted. Greene was buoyed up with happiness. But he was still desperately short of money since his last two books had failed to sell. He approached a number of publications, including *The Times*, his former employer, but his requests for work were turned down flat. He couldn't sleep at night. He began to have doubts about *Stamboul Train*. Then came the news that the Book Society, with a membership of ten thousand readers, had chosen the novel as their Book of the Month for December

1932. Again, Graham's spirits soared. Again they were dashed. Just three days before publication, the best-selling author, J.B Priestley, threatened to sue for libel: he was convinced that the unattractive character of an author in the book was based on him. Graham nearly fainted with fear when he heard he would have to pay damages and costs to Priestley. For the publishers, it was no contest. Heinemann insisted Graham rewrite the offending parts of the text and share the costs of reprinting the novel. Standing in a public phone box, since there was no phone at the cottage, his legs weak with fright, Greene was obliged to recompose part of his story. Thirteen hundred copies of the book had already been printed and bound. The offending twenty pages had to be taken out and replaced. By the time *Stamboul Train* reached the shops, Graham was suffering from nervous exhaustion.

The novel was a great success, but the Greenes continued to be short of money. In 1933, Vivien was pregnant with their daughter, Lucy, later known as Caroline. But hardship and the threat of litigation had changed Graham; his romanticism had disappeared for good, both in his outlook and his writing. He actively looked for freelancing jobs and was asked by Peter Fleming, literary editor of *The Spectator* and brother of the future Bond novelist Ian Fleming, to review for the magazine on a regular basis. Waiting to hear if the film rights for *Stamboul Train* had been sold, thereby ending his financial difficulties, Greene found it almost impossible to work on his next book, *It's a Battlefield*. Then he changed his long-established habit of working in the mornings to the afternoons, and the writer's block left him and he forged ahead with writing his story.

These years of penury had given Greene a very different view of society and now, with the country in the grip of the Depression, his politics veered to the left. His next novel, *England Made Me* (1935), looked at capitalism and how it lurched from one crisis to another, as well as the outdated values of the public school system. He dedicated the book to his wife but, by now, he was seeing prostitutes on a regular basis, in particular a woman called Annette. With the film rights to *Stamboul Train* sold to Twentieth Century Fox, his financial worries eased and the couple moved to a modern luxury flat in Oxford. But Graham never forgot his early struggles as a writer. When he heard how Walter Greenwood, author of *Love on the Dole*, was subsisting on thirty shillings a week, even after the publication of his classic novel, Greene, who had praised the book in a review, asked the Authors' Society to help the novelist. He would later give financial support to Muriel Spark, author of *The Prime of Miss Jean Brodie*, and encourage and help other writers in difficulty.

It was at the reception for his brother Hugh's wedding that Graham mentioned his idea of exploring the Liberian jungle to his twenty-three year-old debutante cousin, Barbara. Both had drunk a lot of champagne and they agreed to make the trip together. Later, when the effects of the bubbly had worn off, both tried to back-peddle, but the commitment had been made. Graham had been restless and was looking for material for a novel; Barbara was enjoying London with her friends and thought the trip would be fun. Greene later called the expedition, during which he nearly died, reckless. Liberia, on the West Coast of Africa, was unchartered territory in those days, where violence and disease were rife. Whole parts of the country were unmapped and the cousins and their native bearers tramped into the sweltering interior on a journey that would change Greene's perspective on life. The romanticism of Victorian exploration gave way to exhaustion, fear and fever. They got lost, encountered several unsavoury characters and situations and, at one point, Graham was so ill with fever that Barbara was sure he would not last the night.

But throughout their trials, the cousins never fell out. Both produced excellent travel accounts of the journey and both were changed by the experience. For Graham, it was the beginning of a life-long love affair with Africa and a need to explore danger zones around the world. Greene's *Journey Without Maps* was published in May 1936, but production was halted over a libel case and not republished until after the war. Peter Fleming, himself an explorer and travel writer, reviewed and admired the book, and compared Graham's writing with Hemingway. Greene's income, although irregular, was much improved and he moved his family to London, to be closer to his work base. Vivien adored the Queen Anne house they rented on Clapham Common and they embarked on a busy social life, making important and useful literary contacts. Graham lectured on his trip to Africa and wrote short stories, including the memorable *The Basement Room*, and another thriller: *A Gun for Sale*. But his writing wasn't generating great sums of money and Vivien was pregnant again.

In 1935, Graham started reviewing films for *The Spectator* in addition to his articles, short stories, lectures and novels. He had always been a film buff but was critical of the puritanical nature of American films, where the censor, as Charlie Chaplin had already discovered, was king at this time. One of his scathing reviews prompted an anonymous letter from High Wycombe: a sheet of paper covered in human excrement. But he continued to criticise films where he felt it was justified and was surprised when Alexander Korda, a producer whose films he had often slated, invited him to write a film script. Greene, like Chaplin, had already worked out that many more people saw films than read books. Graham set to work for eight weeks on his script, *The Green Cockatoo*, at Denham Studios. The result was disastrous but the money was good. The experience put Greene off film writing for a while and he returned to reviewing with a more kindly eye, until the Shirley Temple case landed him in court.

Vivien gave birth to their son, Francis, in September 1936 but, although Graham had a great deal of work, his finances were still stretched. Stressed by his workload and the demands of family life, he began plotting a storyline that would develop into the 'entertainment', *Brighton Rock*. He was now editing a weekly publication, *Night and Day*, that was never to make a profit. He was run down, unable to work with the new baby crying and was covered from head to toe in a nervous rash of boils. He was desperate to escape his situation and planned yet another journey, this time to research a book on the persecution of Catholic priests in Mexico. But putting bread on the table came first, although he did volunteer to go to Spain during the Civil War. In October 1936 he reviewed Shirley Temple's latest film, *Wee Willie Winkie*, and saw the child star's tap-dancing and eye-twinkling as an exercise in coquetry, designed to appeal to middle-aged men. Twentieth

Century Fox sued for libel, his magazine folded and Greene fled to Mexico where he was forced to apologise to all concerned in the case by telegram. He would continue to take pot-shots at what he saw as the down side of American culture, films and politics in his writing over the next few decades, landing himself in even more hot water, and others besides.

Greene found travelling in Mexico in 1938 as difficult and as harsh as Africa had been, and he never fell in love with the country as he had with Liberia. He secretly visited priests who were no longer allowed to celebrate mass, he learned of persecutions and executions and journeyed, sometimes by mule, to the remotest of regions. Weakened by dysentery and made wretched by the heat and dust, he wrote articles for magazines and newspapers while collecting material for what would be his most powerful novel: *The Power and the Glory*, published in 1940. Greene now had the ability to weave his experiences on the playing fields of an English public school into a tale of persecution and betrayal against a backdrop of troubled times in a far-off land. But it was to be another ten years before the story of the wandering whisky priest would be a world best-seller and, by then, Graham would be wandering the world, himself.

George Sanders, Thomas Roe and Dennis Loraine beamed for the television cameras and waved jauntily to the locals. A woman journalist pushed a microphone under Sanders's famous square jaw and addressed him in a broad Scottish accent. 'Is it true, Mr Sanders, that your company intends to build a sausage factory here in Fife?'

George favoured her with a smouldering Hollywood look, then turned to the cameras. 'My colleagues and I have been in high-level talks with the British Board of Trade and the Glenrothes Development Corporation and I am delighted to announce we are expanding our operations already established in the south of England.'

'And how many jobs do you hope to create in this ex-mining community?'

Tom Roe stepped forward, adjusting his glasses. 'We're thinking big here,' he said, importantly. 'The factory will hold up to twenty thousand pigs at a time and we intend to recruit at least two thousand people to keep the plant at full capacity.'

'But what about costs?' asked a tall, thin man in a trench coat, clutching a shorthand notebook.

George Sanders gave the reporter a disdainful smirk before addressing the group of town councillors standing with the journalists and TV crew. 'No need to concern yourselves with details, gentlemen. We are a rock solid company with years of experience in the industry – '

'An' we got names behind us. Famous movie stars. And best-selling writers like Graham – '

'Thank you, Mr Loraine.' Sanders laid a manicured hand on Dennis's arm. 'As I was saying, we don't want to discuss details on this happy occasion – '

'There's a rumour your Sussex factory is two hundred thousand pounds in the red and is about to close,' the trench-coated reporter pressed Sanders again.

'Gentlemen, gentlemen – '

'And you've signed a guarantee with the Royal Bank of Scotland for more than half a million pounds – '

'Ah, now, really – '

'What about the company you started in California, a few years ago? Did the creditors ever get paid? Is that why you moved to Switzerland?'

'I really must insist, gentlemen, that we bring this press conference to an end,' Sanders made a great play of tapping his expensive-looking watch. 'We have meetings to attend and several site surveys while we're here ... Thank you, gentlemen. And lady.' He flashed a debonair smile at the woman journalist and turned and walked quickly from the gathering, followed closely by Roe and Loraine.

Roe tugged at the sleeve of Sanders's cashmere coat as they headed for the waiting Rolls. 'I have to tell you, George, we're running out of money. We owe the British taxpayer over a million ... '

Sanders opened the passenger door of his Rolls for Tom Roe, turned and waved once more for the cameras filming their departure. He affected a small laugh, as if Roe had made some light remark, and growled between his capped teeth. 'We bloody well have to get some money from somewhere, Thomas. You'd better see to it, pretty damned quick, or we'll all be behind bars; your precious celebrity friends included.'

Greene was pleased to be back in London, even though war now seemed inevitable. In Clapham, anti-aircraft guns were ranged on the Common, trenches had appeared and air-raid shelters. The conflict would provide Graham with yet another means of escape from a regular existence, but he continued to worry about money. He knew war would limit the publication of novels and he dreaded being short of cash again. He wrote everything he could:

articles, short stories, novels, plays and reviews; around a quarter of a million words in one year. His nerves were stretched to breaking point and ordinary levels of noise at home, of children and callers and the telephone ringing, led him to look for somewhere he could work without interruption.

He found a studio in Bloomsbury in the heart of London. There, he would write, taking two Benzedrine tablets each day to help him keep to his production target. He was writing an entertainment, *The Confidential Agent*, for quick money in the mornings and *The Power and the Glory* in the afternoons. Soon, the drug made him short-tempered and his marriage suffered. When war was declared, he moved his family out of London, to his parents' house in Sussex, and stayed on, alone, to work in the house on Clapham Common. But he was not really alone, nor was he living on Clapham Common. The long-suffering Vivien had no idea that her marriage was virtually over.

Graham's powerful sex-drive had, until the beginning of the Second World War, been satisfied by his wife and a large number of prostitutes. But, at the outbreak of war, his studio in Bloomsbury became more than just a workplace. He was renting the room from a single woman, Dorothy Glover, and her aged mother. Dorothy was no oil painting: she was short, stout and plain in appearance. But Greene found her outgoing personality and her sense of fun a refreshing change from Vivien's cloying manner. Soon, Dorothy and Graham were passionate lovers. Vivien sensed that her marriage was in danger and told her husband she wanted to return to

London. But Greene moved the family to Oxford and, soon after, the house at Clapham was bombed.

Now that he had forsaken the Benzedrine, Graham was passed fit for active duty and judged by the draft board to be the right material for the Intelligence Service. He was a naturally shy person, reticent and secretive, and disliked chumminess or intimacy with people in general. The board allowed him six months to finish his novels before he was posted to the Ministry of Information. But the organisation seemed to Greene to be a sham ministry in which people did very little but posture and create jobs for themselves. In the Authors' Section, Graham did his best to make the department productive, contacting writers to produce pamphlets to help the war effort. But he was restless, as usual, and wanted to see action. He was to get his wish when the over-populated ministry was scaled down. During the day, he deputised for the Literary Editor of *The Spectator*, who had been called up. Vivien thought her husband had settled down to a steady job, at last. But at night, Greene was in his element, sharing fire-watching duty with Dorothy during the Blitz, dodging bombs and making love in underground shelters. He loved the danger and saw the conflagration as a kind of cleansing of mankind. In his elation, his mood became almost manic.

As an air-raid warden in the West End of London, Greene saw death and destruction on a regular basis, rescuing people who had been buried in the rubble of their homes and recovering the bodies of the dead. Only the theft of his collection of first edition books moved him when his house in Clapham was bombed. He saw the loss of the house as a release from domestic ties and his account of the destruction of a similar house in his short story *The Destructors* moved his wife, who had loved her home, to tears. By now Greene was seeing his family in Oxford only once a month; the marriage was, in all but name, already over. He was in love with Dorothy but continued to visit prostitutes, of which there were many in wartime London. It was a complicated existence but he was soon to be extricated from the situation by his younger sister, Elisabeth.

Graham felt he could contribute more to the war effort than fire-watching and had contacted the SIS (MI6) with a view to becoming an agent. The work appealed to his secretive nature. His sister, who was secretary to the head of the Middle Eastern section, helped push through her brother's application and Graham was vetted for 'Colonial Service' in West Africa. He would be the perfect spy, although he was inept in battle training, couldn't slope arms and damaged two motorcycles before he was excused manoeuvres. But he excelled in intelligence training, learning how to evaluate and approach prospective informants, using information about their past in order to keep a hold on them. He spent a couple of weeks with his family, made his will, collected as many royalties as he could and found a job for his mistress, Dorothy, in his old ministry. In December 1941 he caught the cargo ship to West Africa to begin his career in spying in Freetown, Sierra Leone.

The voyage was an experience in itself. The ship was carrying TNT and in constant danger from submarines. The passengers and crew were a hard-drinking crowd and Graham was rarely sober. Once on dry land, he noted in his diary his impressions of the landscape and the people, and found he despised the snobbery of the colonials. But his time in Sierra Leone would provide him with the backdrop and details for *The Heart of the Matter*, the story of Scobie, a 'colonial' who cannot come to terms with his love life and sees suicide as the only way out.

Graham spent an enjoyable few months training in Lagos while, back in England, Vivien battled with the tax inspector over his royalties: one of the many run-ins Greene would have with the British tax man over the years. He now found plenty of time to write but was sorry to leave Lagos for the heat, dust and vultures of Freetown, his operational base for the next year. There, water was scarce and had to be boiled and disinfected and his accommodation was substandard and full of gigantic ants. In the rainy season, the ground around the house was flooded and the building invaded by flies from the public lavatory across the road. His cover for spying was the vague title of CID officer, but he was rarely seen at police HQ. He collected his telegrams from the headquarters, taking them home to decode and reply to. He drove around in a small Morris car, familiarising himself with the area and looking for potential agents to recruit. The Vichy French were close by, in French Guinea, and part of Graham's job was to search Portuguese boats coming into Freetown harbour for commercial diamonds destined for German arms production.

Greene's supervisor in the SIS was Kim Philby, one of the trio of British double agents who would flee London for Moscow in the early Sixties. Graham was finding it increasingly difficult to work with his immediate boss in Lagos, who seemed intent on sabotaging his best efforts at recruiting agents. Greene loathed being ordered to interrogate suspected German agents and considered it the work of MI5. He would escape up country in his Morris, whenever he could, and immerse himself in writing his psychological thriller, set in London during the Blitz, *The Ministry of Fear*. After a final quarrel with his Lagos superior, Greene resigned his post in Freetown and returned to England in March 1943 where MI6 felt his abilities would be better employed. But he would be returning to the emotional triangle he had left behind in 1941. Dorothy was ever present; nothing had been resolved.

Greene's stage version of *Brighton Rock* opened in Blackpool in 1943 with Richard Attenborough as the evil Pinkie, a part he would play with equal success in the unforgettable film version of the novel. But Graham was now too involved in his intelligence work in London to take on any further scripting commissions. He was living with Dorothy in Bloomsbury while Vivien remained in Oxford with the children, hoping the affair would fizzle out. Then Graham was posted to Philby's intelligence section at Bletchley Park, where MI6 intercepted and decoded German messages and sent out false ones.

Greene's special responsibility was Portugal, a neutral country during the war. But agents on both sides were operating there, including Peter Ustinov's father, Klop Ustinov. Because of his job as press attaché at the German Embassy in 1934, Klop was easily able to identify Nazi intelligence officers who could be recruited to Graham's section. Agent Klop had the Ustinov flair for drama: he would arrange to meet potential contacts in cloak-and-dagger situations, such as a certain tree at the top of a certain mountain. At one point, Klop was told that a German agent was being sent from Madrid to eliminate him. From then on, he was terrified of riding in lifts with other people, convinced someone would stick a lethal needle in him. After the war, his ex-secretary told him she had been asked by German Intelligence to poison him, but she had refused. Klop was to remain in Portugal, working for Graham's section until 1945, recruiting not only Nazi officers but secretaries and desk clerks to British Intelligence.

Meanwhile, Greene's section was transferred to London where he continued to direct agents under the supervision of Kim Philby. Unbeknown to Graham, Philby was frustrating operations as best he could to help the Russian allies. The two men got on well as drinking companions in the pub but their conversation was mostly about work, nothing personal. Graham was more anti-authoritarian than pro-left wing in his beliefs and he was never approached by the Communist Philby. Yet, suddenly, for no apparent reason, he resigned from Philby's section before the Allied invasion in June 1944. Philby had been promoted within the SIS and wanted to take Graham with him. Greene said, later, he felt Philby was building a coterie around him to further his ambitions. Only later would he realise Philby's manipulations were for political, rather than personal, gain.

Graham saw the comical side of spying, too. His tale of Wormold, the vacuum cleaner salesman in *Our Man in Havana*, was based, in part, on the antics of two phoney agents in Portugal and the imaginary contacts they created in order to fool German Intelligence. The first agent, code-named Ostro, used British press reports to give the Abwehr the impression he was running agents in England, Egypt, South Africa, India and America. The section monitored his fake reports but let the messages to the Germans continue; they saw no reason to spoil Ostro's game.

The second agent, code-named Garbo, was a Spaniard living in Lisbon who was determined that Britain should win the war. He fed the Germans tales of a moral breakdown in British society, of drunkenness and greed. Altogether, he invented nearly thirty agents and received payment for them, just as Wormold would do in *Our Man in Havana*. But, whereas Garbo used a *Blue Guide* to the United Kingdom to fabricate his reports to the Abwehr, Wormold simply sent his London paymasters diagrams of vacuum cleaner parts.

Only on one occasion did Philby and Greene share a personal moment, when Graham suffered an internal haemorrhage at the office and Philby took him 'home' in a taxi to Bloomsbury. Dorothy was waiting at the door and whisked Graham inside. Greene asked Philby to keep what he'd seen to himself.

Graham continued to live with Dorothy in London while he worked part-time for the Political Intelligence Unit in Grosvenor Street, as well as the publishers, Eyre and Spottiswoode, as a company director. Greene enjoyed making money and his tax-free entertainment allowance as a director was one good reason to keep him tied to an office job. He actively managed the company and began the publisher's Century Library of forgotten classics and brought François Mauriac to the imprint. But, with the end of the war and the Blitz, Graham became restless and wanted to travel, once more, and write novels full-time. He was less enamoured with Dorothy now but remained with her, rather than return to the domestic ties of Oxford and Vivien. He had hoped the war would have sorted out his love-life and was irritated that it hadn't. He was often depressed or wildly high. He had no idea he was about to meet the greatest love of his life and enter the most productive and creative phase of his writing career. It was his wife who introduced Greene to his muse, and her name was Catherine.

Catherine Walston was an American beauty who turned heads wherever she went. Aged nineteen and bored at college, she had married the wealthy Harry Walston, later Lord Walston, in 1935, twelve years before she met Graham Greene. Outgoing, flirtatious and unconventional, she embraced the good life and a variety of lovers, from priests to the military. She admired Greene's novels and, when she decided to become a Roman Catholic, she wrote to Vivien, asking if Graham would be her godfather. Vivien realised, too late, that Catherine was out to snare Graham, and Walston succeeded, almost immediately. Like Dorothy, Catherine was feisty and independent. And she could afford to be, with a country estate in Cambridgeshire, a cottage in Ireland, a banana plantation in the West Indies and an apartment in Piccadilly, St James's. Graham fell in love with her when she flew him, and the long-suffering Vivien, back from a lunch at the Walston estate in 1947. Dorothy was unhappy about the situation; she had been known to hide Graham's trousers so that he couldn't leave their apartment, or fly into a rage and stab him with her cigarette, leaving burn marks on his hands. But, Vivien quickly understood that Graham's passion for Catherine was much stronger than his attraction to Dorothy had ever been.

Graham's whole personality began to change: he developed a hard shell that was difficult to penetrate. Only Catherine could destabilise him, emotionally. For the next ten years, the lovers would laugh and cry together, quarrel and make love all over the world. Both remained married to their respective partners but Greene and Walston went through an unofficial marriage ceremony that bound them in a special way. During their years together, Graham was inspired to write such classics as *The Heart of the Matter, Our Man in Havana, The Third Man, The Quiet American* and the story based on their turbulent relationship, The *End of the Affair.* He would continue to support Dorothy financially until she died an alcoholic in 1971. He would also support Vivien but the couple separated in 1948, at the height of his affair with Catherine.

Graham took an apartment next door to the Walstons' London home and was often a guest at their country house, until he was finally banned by Harry from seeing Catherine there. Graham often pleaded with Catherine to leave Walston, but she knew from the beginning that her husband was the more stable of the two men. The couple had five children, and Harry was on his way to becoming a life peer. Walston also had discreet affairs of his own and was tolerant of his wife's amours. Graham would lose his temper and create terrible scenes in an attempt to prise Catherine from her wealthy and secure existence. He bought a retreat on Anacapri, on the

Italian Amalfi coast, where they spent many happy holidays but, always, Catherine returned to Harry.

Graham's moods would swing from great highs to deep depressions, depending on how much time he could spend with Catherine. His novel *The Heart of the Matter*, written just after Greene had fallen in love with her, showed a man driven to suicide by his obligations to his wife and his passion for his mistress. He hardly noticed the beautiful actress, Alida Valli, in Alexander Korda and Carol Reed's version of his story *The Third Man* because he was longing to return from filming in Vienna to Catherine. Korda and Reed had already brought Greene's gripping short story *The Fallen Idol* to the screen and the producer, Korda, like Greene, had worked for the SIS during the war. The two men became close friends and both continued their affiliation to MI6 for the rest of their lives.

Graham was now the successful author he had striven to become, but he hated the celebrity status, being hounded by autograph hunters at airports and bothered by people who wanted to make conversation wherever he went. He had taken to travel again to relieve the depressions he experienced when parted from Catherine. He was obsessed by her and dedicated his novel *The End of the Affair* (1951) 'To C'. The story mirrored several aspects of their relationship and the main characters in the book were unquestionably modelled on Greene, Catherine and her husband, Harry. *The End of the Affair* did not have a happy ending, but Graham applauded Deborah Kerr, his future neighbour in Switzerland, for her role as Sarah in the Hollywood film version of the story in 1953.

Greene wandered the globe throughout the fifties, seeking out dangerous situations, prostitutes and opium dens in an effort to forget Catherine. He spent time in Malaya, reporting on the Communist uprising there, and went on to Indo-China and the troubles in Vietnam that would inspire him to write *The Quiet American* (1955), a criticism of American foreign policy and the CIA. In Kenya, he experienced the settlers' terror behind their barricades during the Mau Mau uprising, but it was the rise of McCarthyism in America in the early fifties that landed Graham in a real trouble spot. His student membership of the Communist Party for a few weeks at Oxford led to him being denied an entry visa for the United States where he needed to work. Greene decided to use his fame as a novelist to make the situation headline news around the world. The U.S. authorities eventually backed down, but only gave him a short stay visa. Graham was incensed. In Hollywood, he had drinks with Charlie Chaplin, who would later become a good friend, and learned just how far the McCarthy hunt for suspected Communists was ruining the lives of writers and artists. When Chaplin, himself, was denied re-entry into the States in 1952, having lived and worked in the country for decades, entertaining millions of Americans, Graham wrote an open letter to Charlie in the *New Statesman*, reprinted in *New Republic*, supporting the world's best-loved comedian and criticising those who sought to ostracise him. When Greene applied for a further visa, he was given one for an eight-week stay only.

But Graham continued to speak up for those he felt were being treated unfairly. In 1955, he picked *Lolita* as one of the three best books of the year in his review in *The*

Sunday Times. Nabokov's novel had been panned by critics as being virtually pornographic, but Greene championed the work again, in 1956, in the *New York Times Book Review*. The book became a worldwide success, and so did the film of the novel. A few years later, Nabokov moved to Switzerland and installed himself permanently in the Montreux Palace Hotel, just a few kilometres along the lake from the small apartment where Greene would live.

Graham's love for Catherine continued unabated for the best part of a decade. When the Walstons moved apartment to the exclusive Albany in Piccadilly, Greene took an apartment there, too. He would meet Catherine in exotic locations, as well as his retreat in Anacapri and in London. The lovers holidayed at Firefly, Noël Coward's home in Jamaica. Later, Graham would stay at Firefly with other women, as well. He had a serious affair with the beautiful Swedish actress, Anita Björk, in the late 1950's and it was possible that the intended suicide of a character in one of his plays cost him the Nobel Prize for Literature. A number of Swedish writers were offended that the suicide attempt in the play mirrored the successful one by Anita's late husband. Whatever the reason, he was passed over by the Swedish Academy, and many believed the oversight was deliberate, including Graham, himself.

Noël Coward had become a good friend of Greene's and starred with Alec Guinness in the 1959 film version of *Our Man in Havana*. After filming, Coward purchased a luxury home on the Swiss Riviera for tax reasons, joining Charlie Chaplin and other British and American actors and writers, ahead of Greene. But Noël Coward, too, would fall under the spell of the affable Lausanne lawyer, Thomas Roe, though he survived what he called a 'rip-snorter' of an affair, the scandal of Royal Victoria Sausages Limited.

Thomas Roe sat in his Lausanne office and surveyed the contents of three open packages on his desk. He picked up one of the hundred dollar bills with the tips of his fingers, carefully examined both sides and threw it down in disgust. He buzzed his secretary to get him Dennis Loraine in Los Angeles. As he waited for the call, he pushed a few of the notes around the desk with his pen, frowning as he did so. The phone jingled and Roe picked it up immediately. He didn't waste time with niceties. 'Dennis, what the bloody hell have you sent me? These bills are Bank of Toyland - I wouldn't get them past a four year-old! What do you expect me to do with this crap? We're in serious trouble, here!'

"Ere, 'old up, matey!' Loraine sounded hurt. 'I done me best, 'aven't I? George said we 'ad a licence to print money, an' we 'ave. Bill numbers a bit smudged, yeah. They done a rush job. But half a mill's better than nuffink! You only gotta pay for the good ones, not the duds – '

Roe's voice was low and sounded desperate. 'Dennis, I told you I need one million dollars, fast.' He picked up another note and rubbed it between his fingers. 'The paper's all wrong. It's rubbish. I'll never get it cashed ... ' He could hear muffled talk at Loraine's end. Dennis sounded conciliatory, the other voice was insistent.

'Right then, me old china, this is what you do. Best not to pass the bills. Might get traced back. Use 'em as collateral – '

'You idiot! I have to change them. I need the cash!' Roe let out an exasperated sigh. 'Look, I'll call you back when I've been to Geneva. Let you know how it went.'

"Ere, 'old up, Tom! Just a minute! Just a bleedin' –' The phone line went dead. Loraine stared at the mouthpiece for a moment, then at his companion.

By the end of the 1950's, Greene was famous, wealthy and a high-flying businessman. He was generous with his money but careful to avoid the tax man with as many schemes as he could. As a publisher, before the war, he had helped the writer James Hadley Chase, author of *No Orchids for Miss Blandish* and other racy best-sellers, to become a top story-writer, not only in Britain but in France where he'd introduced Chase to his Paris agent. Chase would move to the lakeside village of Corseaux, just outside Vevey, on the Swiss Riviera, and knew Thomas Roe well; their wives were close.

Roe, originally a solicitor, had distinguished himself in military administration in the Middle East during the war and had received an OBE, followed by a CBE, for his organisational skills in the run-up to Independence in India. Returning to England, Roe quickly saw the financial opportunities to be had from the newly-formed European Common Market. Cross-border tax avoidance for wealthy clients became Roe's speciality, with special reference to Switzerland and Liechtenstein. In Lausanne, Roe joined forces with Hollywood matinée idol George Sanders and small-time crook Denis Loraine, also known as Denis Edwards. If Loraine had form, George Sanders had history. Sanders loathed the Hollywood film business and dreamed of becoming an international businessman, never to set foot in front of a camera again. His first venture, in California in 1956, lost him, and several of his friends, every penny they had invested. Sanders's house, car and bank accounts were seized and he fled to Switzerland.

Sanders, Roe and Loraine were soon in business, investing the capital of the wealthy and famous in a number of projects with little or no substance. They succeeded for a while because Sanders was a silken-tongued front man, Roe had clients and their money on an international scale and Loraine was skilled at massaging accounting figures. The Royal Victoria Sausage Company was one of many schemes, including film-making, oil and property, dreamed up by the trio to fund their high-life. On the darker side was a money-laundering set-up and a Mafia connection. The CIA, Interpol and the Swiss police were watching and waiting.

Graham Greene was thinking seriously about retirement. His novel, *A Burnt Out Case* (1961) reflected his ennui and he was sure he would never write another book. He was now a director of the successful publishing house, Bodley Head, and spent part of his time in the office following his investments in the stock market. Then a trip to Haiti, where the ruthless dictator, Papa Doc, reigned with his vicious army of Tontons Macoute, energised him. Another story emerged from his ever-active imagination, but it would take several years for him to produce the novel, *The Comedians*. He bought himself a flat in Paris and met a petite French lady in Cameroon,

West Africa. The trouble was the Inland Revenue was continually demanding unreasonable sums of money from him. When a relative, to whom he had ceded a small copyright, died, Graham found himself liable for outrageously projected earnings from the work. He was more than ready to fall in with Thomas Roe's tax-avoidance schemes and he put himself almost completely in Roe's hands.

Greene was not even a director of his Swiss company. All his foreign earnings went through Roe's hands, and much more besides. Roe kept all Graham's confidential papers in his office and, as nominal director, invested Greene's money on his behalf. Graham contented himself with an annual salary. After all, he would be retired soon. He could not, and would not, believe that Thomas Roe was a crook, even as the evidence began to mount against him in the early 1960's. Greene hung on to his dream of retirement, but life was becoming stranger than his fiction.

The Royal Victoria Sausage Company had been formed in England in 1961. A factory for sausage-making was acquired in Horsham, Sussex, but it did not make sausages, or money. However, Roe's ability to sniff out new sources of cash for the trio led him to the British Board of Trade and the availability of regional grants from the Scottish office. The former mining town of Glenrothes on the East Coast of Scotland needed new industry to reduce unemployment, and the management of the sausage enterprise was hundreds of thousands of pounds in the red and needed a quick fix. By 1963, money was being thrown at the company: the Royal Bank of Scotland loaned them around half a million pounds which, added to funds from the development corporation, amounted to somewhere near a million pounds, plus another half a million from private investors like Graham Greene.

The trio went on a spending spree. Italy, where Roe and Loraine seemed to know the right politicians, became the next area of activity. One film-making project after another lost money. Luxury offices in Rome, backhanders to oil the wheels of officialdom and a private jet to whisk clients and starlets from one lavish party to another soon ate into the sausage company's money. By the end of 1964, the Royal Victoria Sausage Company was bankrupt. The Board of Trade was obliged to investigate. Graham Greene was one of many summoned by the Board to answer questions. Even then, Graham refused to believe he could have been so wrong about the genial Mr Roe.

In a series of press interviews in Greene's Albany flat in 1965, Roe insisted he was the victim of a scam. He had been duped, he said, by others. He even offered to guarantee some of Graham's money, personally; not that he had a penny, dime or centime to his name. It was James Hadley Chase who finally rang the alarm bells. In July 1965, Thomas Roe visited several banks in Geneva, attempting to cash counterfeit dollar bills. The Swiss police arrested him on the Geneva-Lausanne autoroute and searched his office and home. His bewildered and frightened wife phoned Chase's wife. Chase immediately retrieved his money from Roe and telephoned Graham to warn him. Greene was uneasy but not about to be panicked; it was all a mistake, he was sure. Roe was an international lawyer. His clients were Graham's friends: Charlie Chaplin, Noël Coward and James Hadley Chase, and there were others, in Hollywood: William Holden and

Robert Mitchum, and what about that fellow, the forties' matinée idol, George Sanders?

On 4 August 1965, Thomas Roe was charged with fraud in Switzerland. The next day, Denis Loraine was arrested in Los Angeles and charged with offences involving counterfeit money. Questions were asked in the Houses of Parliament, but the loss to the British taxpayer was quietly buried by the British Government. Both Roe and Loraine served prison sentences while George Sanders returned to California and declared himself bankrupt. Sanders later committed suicide in a hotel room in Barcelona, having lost everything.

But Greene, who had lost nearly everything, had no intention of killing himself. The attractive French woman he had met in Douala had returned to France and was living in Juan-les-Pins. But he was deeply worried there would be an investigation into his financial affairs; all his papers had been seized in the raid on Tom Roe's offices and home in Lausanne. There was only one thing he could do to avoid punitive taxes: he had to become a tax exile, a resident abroad. An agreement was finally reached with the Inland Revenue. Graham had to leave the UK, for good, by New Year's Day 1966. After a farewell party with close friends at the Connaught Hotel in London on 31 December 1965, Graham caught the cross-channel ferry to France. He would never live in England again, but he looked forward, not back. His affair with the woman who would partner him for the rest of his life was now well-established. He was entering a new phase in his life.

Greene's first objective was to recoup his financial losses. All thoughts of retirement went out of the window; work was the thing. He set up another tax company in

Switzerland, this time with a bona fide lawyer. *The Comedians* (1966) was not only a successful novel but MGM turned the story into a star-studded film. Richard Burton, Elizabeth Taylor, Peter Ustinov and Alec Guinness played the main characters, filming on location in Dahomey, then at the Victorine film studios in the South of France. It would be the last time Graham would write the screenplay of one of his novels, but he was delighted to return to the studios as an actor, playing the part of an English insurance agent in François Truffaut's celebrated *Day for Night* (1973). Truffaut could hardly believe that Greene was not a real actor, so professional was his performance before the camera. But Graham was an infinitely more relaxed person now. He had moved to Antibes to be near the woman who had brought a new stability to his life. Her name was Yvonne Cloetta.

The sale to MGM of the film rights for *The Comedians* enabled Greene to buy a modest two-roomed apartment, overlooking the busy harbour at Antibes. Every day, after he had finished his regular morning stint of writing, Yvonne Cloetta would drive over, from her house in Juan-les-Pins, to have lunch with Graham in one of the excellent harbour restaurants, before returning with him to his apartment for the afternoon. Yvonne's marriage, like that of Catherine Walston's, had broken down but continued for the sake of the children. Yvonne had two daughters, to whom Graham became close. But the protectiveness Greene came to feel for her children would lead to one of the major confrontations in his life.

Graham was enjoying himself again, writing and travelling, often in South America, a location he used for his taut novel *The Honorary Consul* (1973). He visited

Russia and met up with Kim Philby again. He did not agree with Philby's politics but understood the double agent's commitment to his cause. In his novel, *The Human Factor* (1978), Greene would look objectively at Philby's situation. Graham also visited England occasionally. He returned for twenty-four hours in March 1966 to receive a CBE from the Queen, possibly for his intelligence work; he had already turned down a knighthood. In 1978, after several years of ill-health, Catherine Walston died of cancer and was buried near her country home. Graham had wanted to visit her in a London clinic, knowing she was dying. But Catherine, her looks now faded, preferred her former lover to remember her as she had been. Greene filled a taxi with flowers and watched it depart for the clinic. Catherine had been at the centre of the most turbulent and productive period of his life. There were fewer reasons for him to visit England now. He continued writing short stories, articles and two volumes of autobiography: *A Sort of Life* (1971) and *Ways of Escape* (1980). What energy he had left was channelled into his last major battle with authority. This time he took on the Mayor of Nice.

When Yvonne's eldest daughter, Martine, endured a painful divorce, Graham pitched in to support her, seeing himself, as usual, on the side of the underdog. But Martine's husband had powerful connections on the French Riviera, all the way up to the flamboyant Mayor of Nice, Jacques Médecin. Greene's pamphlet, *J'Accuse* (1982) was his protest, in the fashion of Emile Zola's defence of the accused in the famous Dreyfus affair, at Martine's treatment, in and out of court. He used whatever clout he had, writing to newspapers and the

French government; even handing in his Chevalier of the Legion of Honour medal, which was promptly returned to him. He accused Nice and its right-wing mayor of corruption and advised tourists not to visit the town. He was threatened with violence, taken to court and accused of libel and invasion of privacy. His pamphlet was seized and he lost the court case. He was now in his late seventies, ill and exhausted. He'd had operations for Dupuytren's disease on his left hand, refusing to undergo surgery for his right hand as it would have prevented him writing for three months, and, more seriously, an operation for cancer of the colon in 1979. It would be 1990 before Médecin's reign of corruption was exposed. The mayor fled France and was arrested in Uruguay, in South America, and brought back to face charges.

Graham saw Martine safely settled in Switzerland, close to where his daughter, Lucy Caroline, was living on the Swiss Riviera. But his health was failing. His last trips to Moscow were the international Peace Conference in 1987, where he shared the stage with Mikhail Gorbachev, a man Greene much admired, followed by a final visit with Yvonne in 1988 to comfort Kim Philby's widow, Rufina. His chairmanship of a literary prize in Ireland seemed to take the last of his energy; he would not be seen at a public event again. In Switzerland, for Christmas and the New Year with his daughter, he was hospitalised twice. It was discovered that he had leukaemia. He needed regular blood transfusions.

Those closest to Graham felt it best that he live in Switzerland on a permanent basis so, in 1989, he and Yvonne moved into a modest apartment at Chemin du Châno 26 in the village of Corseaux, near Vevey, on Lake

Geneva. It was a wine-growing area Greene knew well: his daughter lived close by, as did Yvonne's daughter, Martine. His old friend, Charlie Chaplin had been buried, and re-buried, nearby and his good friend, James Hadley Chase had lived in Corseaux until his death in 1985. In 1984, Graham had been saddened by the death of another friend who'd lived in the village: the actor James Mason. Mason had starred in the film version of Greene's study of wealth and greed, the novel *Doctor Fischer of Geneva and the Bomb Party* (1980). The film had been shot around Lake Geneva in the depths of winter, and James Mason was not a well man. Graham watched the night scenes being filmed in the open air, in freezing Swiss temperatures, and was impressed, not only by Mason's acting but his uncomplaining application to his work and his consideration for others. Mason died shortly afterwards of heart disease in a Lausanne hospital, but it was to be many years before the actor's ashes would be scattered, close to their mutual friend Charlie Chaplin.

Meanwhile, Graham was fighting his own declining health, chained, as he saw himself, by tubes and wires to the blood transfusion apparatus at the local hospital in Vevey. But the transfusions were no longer working. His mind was sometimes clouded. He slipped and fell on the winter ice outside the apartment in Corseaux. Only the support of his mistress for over thirty years, Yvonne Cloetta, was keeping him going.

One of the first things Greene noticed when he moved to Corseaux in September 1990 was how quiet it was, compared with the bustling harbour at Antibes. He knew, even then, that he was dying and would always need medication and regular transfusions. Graham had abandoned his faith in his middle years and, now, he wanted the comfort of belief again. His old friend, Father Leopoldo Duran, with whom he had travelled around Portugal and North-West Spain, discussing philosophy and religion and sampling local wines, had inspired Greene's novel *Monsignor Quixote* in 1982. Now, each time Father Duran spoke to Graham by phone from Spain, the writer's voice was a little weaker, and there were occasions when Greene was totally drained of energy and unable to talk anyone. Sheer willpower enabled him to complete his one hundred paces around the flat each day. He had given up writing and was reading much less. But, always the observer, Graham found the experience of dying an interesting one, and wondered if there was life after death. He hoped there was, he told Yvonne, so that he could continue to help other writers, as he had done throughout his career.

Graham chose a double burial plot among the hillside vineyards of Corseaux, a stone's throw from the cemetery at Corsier-sur-Vevey, where Charlie Chaplin had been laid to rest. He was ready, he said, to leave this world. He became impatient; why was it taking so long? In his first floor room in L'Hôpital de la Providence in Vevey, early in April 1991, Graham was aware he was slipping away. Father Duran arrived from Spain and administered the last rites. The hospital doctors were amazed at Graham's serenity. But Greene saw death as a beginning. He held Yvonne's hand, waiting for the end, closed his eyes and slipped into a coma.

On Wednesday 3 April 1991, at 11.40 a.m., Graham Greene passed peacefully to the other side. He left behind a flurry of activity: Buckingham Palace had to be informed of his death, since he had received the honour of a CBE from Her Majesty. The funeral would be a formal one: the British Ambassador would attend, Graham's family, his friends and, of course, the press. After the church service in Corseaux, Vivien Greene stood and watched, Yvonne just behind her, as the dark wood coffin was lowered into the ground in the small cemetery on the hillside. Yvonne never stopped loving Greene. She kept their apartment in the village and tended Graham's grave until her own death in 2001.

In the film version of Greene's story *The Third Man*, the actor Orson Welles added his own observation that the Swiss have enjoyed hundreds of years of peace and democracy. And what have they produced? he asks Joseph Cotten. Cuckoo clocks! Graham Greene would have disagreed. Greene and fellow artists, such as James Mason, Vladimir Nabokov, Charlie Chaplin and Georges Simenon, spent the final years of their colourful, often dramatic, lives against a backdrop of Swiss mountains and pretty villages, but their reasons for making a home in Switzerland had nothing to do with cuckoo clocks, and everything to do with wanting the best in life.

Chapter 4

George Sanders and James Mason

'**M**y dear James, the whole thing is simply a licence to print money,' drawled Sanders, matter-of-factly, down the phone.

To James Mason, struggling actor, newly-arrived in Hollywood after the war, George's words were the lifeline he'd been praying for. 'Well, I ... ' Mason strove to find the right words. He didn't want to appear desperate. 'I can certainly use my knowledge and experience. I gained a First, you know, in Architecture, at Cambridge in Thirty-one.'

Sanders gave a short laugh. 'Not necessary, old boy. I don't intend for us to *work* for a living. That would be just too boring. Perhaps sing for our supper a little, if you know what I mean. Some of these wealthy ladies are very attractive ... '

'Oh, I'm happy to design their houses for them,' James assured him, wondering what his wife would say about the project. Pamela had ambitions for her husband in other directions, he knew. 'It might be rather nice to get back to the drawing board, after so long. I – '

'No need, old chap, really! I have my contacts ... ' George lowered his voice. 'Between you and me, old man, one ex-pat actor to another and all that, I'm rather close to Mrs Conrad Hilton, these days. And she knows just about everyone with money - '

'Zsa Zsa Gabor?'

'Delightful lady. In touch with the business world, that's the thing. Not this ridiculous posturing called acting – '

'I want to act,' Mason interrupted him. 'But properly. I didn't come all the way from England for this studio system rubbish. I want control over my career.'

'Well, you won't get it here, mincing around with this bloody English Colony lot. And you won't make much money, either. Property's the thing, old boy. Trust me. Safe as houses. Can't fail. Now, this is the plan ... '

Both George Sanders and James Neville Mason were born into the genteel world of privilege of the early 1900s; George in 1906 and James in 1909. But, whereas Sanders spent a happy childhood in St. Petersburg in the years before the Bolshevik Revolution scattered the Russian ruling class across the globe, James Mason enjoyed a comfortable and stable home life in the industrial north of England, in the West Riding of Yorkshire.

James was the youngest of three boys born in fairly quick succession in 1906, 1907 and 1909 to successful Huddersfield textile merchant John Mason and his cultured wife Mabel. His father's cloth business ensured that the boys were brought up in a large house with a cook, maid, gardener and, of course, that mainstay of every Edwardian nursery, the nanny. Like all upper middle-class boys, Rex, Colin and James Mason found, as they grew older, their nanny was replaced by a governess until they were ready to go to boarding school. Their preparatory school at Windemere was in the heart of the Lake District, surrounded by spectacular views of rolling hills and deep lakes but where it always seemed to rain. James, the quietest of the three boys, appeared to enjoy his three years at Windemere prep before following his brothers to Marlborough public school. There, though he was no great academic, he always seemed to gain reasonable marks in class.

Mason's early passion was photography, not acting. He also learned the flute, which he would enjoy playing again in later years and, like all public school boys, he was obliged to play rugby football in winter temperatures and all weathers. His interest in photography led his grandfather to send him a monthly magazine: *Play Pictorial*. The photographs of actors and actresses, the plays they were in and the theatre reviews, all must have lodged in James's subconscious. The magazine provided light relief from academic text books and a certain amount of glamour for the boy, and London seemed to him to be a city well worth visiting.

Meanwhile, the young George Sanders and his brother, Tom, were enjoying their summer holidays in England. It was the sea that fired George's imagination. He would be an English sailor when he grew up, he once told Grand Duke Michael over tea. But his idyllic childhood was about to end. At the outbreak of the First World War in 1914, George's father, knowing life in Russia was about to change forever, sent the family to England. After prep school, George and his brother were sent to Bedales boarding school where George felt himself to be a foreigner, an outsider. When the Sanders family lost everything they had in the Russian revolution that followed the war in 1917, they remained in England. They were now dependent on relatives for financial support, a situation that would colour George's frustrated outlook on life and fuel his need for wealth, status and independence. Soon, he retreated behind a mask of contempt and disdain for those around him and adopted the behaviour of an English upper-class cad.

Any boy who appeared to be above himself at Marlborough school was thrown, in full school uniform, into the swimming pool. After this happened to Mason tertius, as the youngest Mason boy was known, James grew into a reserved and studious gentleman, headed for university to study the Classics. But the family wealth was contracting: the General Strike and the gathering economic Depression were affecting the British textile manufacturing business. James left Marlborough in the summer of 1928, bound for Cambridge University to study for a post in the Civil Service. There was no point in him joining the ailing family business now, his father made that clear.

George Sanders was about to enter the University of Life. The only happiness he and his brother would know at Bedales was acting in the school plays, and George discovered he had a talent for sketching. When his brother was expelled from Bedales, George followed him to Brighton College where he was a prize-winning student and sportsman, in spite of his later insistence that the institution was a dull place. There, he sang in college concerts and was active in the Officers' Training Corps. A boxing champion at six foot three inches and weighing in at two hundred pounds, the world should have been his oyster. But the brothers were continually short of cash because of the dire situation of their family's finances and the boys were embarrassed by their too-small and out-of-mode clothes. Sanders would never forget the financial insecurity he suffered at this time.

It was assumed by the Mason family that James would graduate from Cambridge and join the Indian Civil Service: a respectable job for a young man in the early nineteen-thirties. But, in his first year at university, James discovered river boats and rowing regattas. It was a rowing pal who first got him interested in student amateur dramatics, where James soon felt he'd acquitted himself with some success. Something had stirred in James's normally amiable character: a sense of self, a spirit of defiance. To his father's horror, he quit studying Classics and switched to Architecture. He'd always enjoyed sketching and now he worked furiously to make up for lost course time, even sacrificing amateur theatricals until his final year. James left Cambridge with one of only three

Firsts in Architecture awarded by the University in 1931. But the Depression now gripped the nation. No one was building anything. No one needed an architect; least of all, an inexperienced trainee architect.

George Sanders arrived in South America at the beginning of 1926 for what was to be the happiest four years of his life. As a sales representative for the British and American Tobacco Company, he grew to love Argentina, its culture, language and people, and would sing their songs and play the guitar and dance the tango. He enjoyed putting on theatricals in mining camps to advertise his company's products. And he loved South American women. It was while he was staying with an attractive widow in Chile that her fiancé called one evening, after George and the lady had retired to spend the night together. Challenged to a duel, there and then, George leaped out of the bedroom window with a pistol, ready to do battle on the gravel with the cuckolded fiancé. In the dark, the two men jostled blindly to arrange themselves back to back before walking the regulation ten paces away from each other. But George was still barefoot, straight from the widow's bed, and when he heard the other man's footsteps cease on the gravel, he quickly turned and fired. No shot was returned. The fiancé lay bleeding on the ground, though, to Sanders's relief, not mortally wounded. George was promptly arrested, jailed, fired from his job and deported back to England.

Acting seemed like a good idea to James Mason. He'd enjoyed the amateur theatricals at Cambridge and felt he had a good chance of finding employment in London. Together with an old university pal, he took a small rented room in Chelsea and began pounding the pavements, looking for work. But he lacked professional experience and stage doors were closed to him. He sent off hundreds of job applications to advertisers in *The Stage*, but the response was always the same. Desperately short of money by the autumn of 1931, he was finally taken on by a touring company who promised to pay him a small wage if box office takings allowed. James Mason made his professional acting debut in Aldershot, just as the infant Charlie Chaplin had done when his mother had dried on stage in the 1890's and where the young David Niven first trod the boards in 1928. The tour moved on to Tiverton, then Bath and Bilston in the north where the company's funds ran out and James was obliged to return home, penniless, for Christmas. At least he could now call himself a professional actor.

Mason soon joined other theatre companies and gained more experience, even if the pay was minimal and he lived constantly on the breadline. But, in a world of footlights and playing to the gallery, he was an unusually quiet, reserved sort of actor. Onstage and off, he seemed drawn to women with a stronger character than his own, allowing them to take the leading role in social situations. He was not, and never would be, very relaxed in company; more than one fellow actor saw tension and moodiness in his behaviour off-duty. Finally, after a stint at the Old Vic, James secured a week's work in an Alexander Korda picture at Denham Studios. But the taciturn, glowering James and the film's swashbuckling star, Douglas Fairbanks, took an instant dislike to each other and, after three days on the set, Mason was quietly asked to leave the picture.

But the camera loved his icy good looks and his velvet, cultured tone of voice and he was soon finding regular work in British 'B' movies. It was during the making of his third film that he first set eyes on, or rather, experienced the strong presence of a cameraman's wife, Pamela Kellino. The beautiful Pamela had arrived on the set one evening to object to her husband, Roy, working late on the film. She was the daughter of one of the Osterer brothers who handled the film distribution at Gaumont-British and, therefore, half the cinemas in Britain. Soon, James was lodging with the Kellinos, ostensibly to save money, and was rarely apart from Pamela. Occasionally, Roy would ask James to leave, but Mason would be back the next day. They made an odd trio but Roy and James remained friends, although their friendship was tested when Pamela and Roy finally divorced. James married Pamela in 1941.

A fellow actor at the Fox studio in Wembley was contract player, George Sanders. He had returned to London from South America and finally found work in an advertising office, where he'd spent most of his time entertaining his office colleagues, including an attractive redhead called Greer Garson. When George was sacked for not concentrating on his work, the future looked bleak again. However, the office redhead had been impressed by Sanders's entertainments and took him along to her amateur theatrical group while his uncle paid to have his voice trained. Greer Garson was signed by MGM and went to the United States in 1937. George sang and played the piano and guitar in nightclubs and took roles in BBC radio plays before landing a part in Noël Coward's successful *Conversation Piece*. After good reviews in other plays, he began to get small parts in films and soon developed the world-weary, sneering persona that seemed to distance him intellectually from other characters on screen.

George found film acting an undemanding occupation and his disdain for his work showed in the haughty demeanour he brought to his roles. He signed a long-term contract with British and Dominion film studio which, after a studio fire, was sold to Twentieth Century Fox and took him to Hollywood in 1936. There, he specialised in cold, elegant, villainous characters and played the parts to perfection, to such an extent that refined villainy almost became second nature to Sanders.

James Mason's aloofness and general contempt for the way British studios were run in the 1930's seeped into the characters he played on screen. He craved artistic freedom and the opportunity to make his own films, but was hampered by a lack of money. He quarrelled with producers and wrote indignant articles in the press, criticising the British film industry; in effect, biting the hand he had hoped would feed him. He was never offered a contract or work in Hollywood, for Mason was seen as a difficult actor by studio bosses and technicians. James's frustration with his situation boiled over into his memorable roles as a wicked Regency rake in several Rank movies. He dismissed his parts in these costume romps, but they made him a star. His moodiness on screen was seen as masterful and sexy by cinema-goers but, in reality, the glint in Mason's eye that the camera loved was pent-up anger and exasperation for the situation he found himself in. Whether it was his declared wartime pacifism or the fact that he was living with Pamela, a married woman, James's conduct and outspokenness about his own industry did him no favours. By the end of the war, he was obliged to look to America for an artistic escape route.

In his own contemptuous way, George Sanders was enjoying Hollywood. There were opportunities to be had, not just in the movie industry which he'd always found difficult to take seriously, or the attractive women who were a pleasant enough diversion, but in the business world where Sanders believed the road to success and its attendant wealth really lay. By the late 1930's, he was playing the lead in most of his movies, virtually cornering the market in suave villains. But he disliked the Hollywood social scene and preferred sailing his sloop or reading a good book to being seen in the latest nightclub. And he didn't like spending money if he could help it. The lack of funds in his teenage years and the social embarrassment it had caused him left him with a permanent fear of being short of money. This led, in turn, to an obsession with making a fortune by the most direct route, with a view to retiring from the world.

George had married a pretty blonde 'B' movie actress called Susan Larson in 1940, but he kept the news from the press. Susan, a demure 25 year-old, stayed at home, out of the limelight, while George continued to work in films, promoting his caddish, bachelor image. Sanders was never seen with his wife at Hollywood socials and, even when questioned by reporters, denied that he was married. He was a difficult husband, intellectually gifted, while Susan was not well-educated or mentally strong. Timid and tearful, she eventually had a nervous breakdown and left the marital home. Her mental collapse was a complete surprise to George, who sought help from a psychiatrist while their divorce went through. He had begun, too late, to appreciate Susan: his quiet, unassuming 'rock', the butt of his scathing remarks at home. She had provided a solid background while he'd focussed on his career, not his marriage. His Hollywood status was riding high and he was at the peak of his popularity. But, with Susan's departure in 1946, George found he was no longer interested in being a film star. He wanted to retire, withdraw from the movie world and satisfy his intellectual interests. He began to look around for business opportunities as a way of making a fast buck.

James and Pamela Mason arrived in New York at the end of 1946 with their entourage of domestics and a number of household pets. But, in spite of his box office success in British films such as *Odd Man Out, The Wicked Lady* and *The Seventh Veil* with Anne Todd, it was difficult for James to find work. He was embroiled in a legal battle with his ex-manager who was demanding a large cut of any work Mason took. James, backed by the feisty Pamela, chose to fight the court case, but it meant he could not work for a year. Short of money and tied to New York by the court case, Mason turned to journalism to earn some cash. But the criticism in his articles of the Hollywood system did nothing to further his career. He and Pamela wrote a book about their beloved cats and acted in a play which flopped in Philadelphia. Money was running out fast. They were obliged to head for California where James hid in their rented home to avoid being served another writ by the ex-manager.

After a year of unemployment and the court case settled, Mason had to abandon his artistic principles and take any passable job on offer. Apart from the cost of running a large household with its permanent guests, including Pamela's ex-husband, there was now a baby on the way. But James would never feel comfortable with the razzmatazz of Hollywood, whereas Pamela loved every aspect of Californian life. James seemed to become quieter, more introverted, during these Hollywood years while Pamela became the sociable party-giver. Yet, in spite of his wife's best efforts at networking, Mason could not land the parts that would bring him box office success or, more to the point, financial success. And he needed both, more than ever, now that he'd purchased Buster Keaton's old Hollywood home. Then, one day, the phone rang. It was his good friend, George, asking how he was 'placed' these days.

Mason was happy to share his discontents with a like-minded actor. Sanders and Mason, both suave intellectuals with cultured English voices, were often up for the same roles: usually the villain in the film. But Sanders had tired of film industry, particularly its social scene. Mason also loathed socialising with the Hollywood set, especially a group of actors known as the 'English Colony', and was beginning to think he had made a mistake in leaving England and his solid career there. Sanders proposed they devote their energies to the property business, providing luxury mansions for well-heeled widows and raking in enormous fees for putting on the charm. James was up for it and was happy to design the properties himself. It would make a welcome change from the demands of tinsel-town and would stretch him intellectually. Plans were laid and Sanders allowed himself to be wooed by the wealthy Mrs Conrad Hilton, alias the Hungarian actress, Zsa Zsa Gabor. In 1949, George, still unhappy with the direction his life was taking, and the bubbly Zsa Zsa began their tempestuous marriage. Meanwhile, decent film offers finally began to come James's way.

The marriage to Zsa Zsa lasted only a few years. As his wife's acting career flourished, George became moody and unsettled. He would often move out of their apartment, taking his grand piano with him, then returning when he felt like it. He could be witty and charming and, with his trained singing voice, he could entertain friends for hours. He made a number of record albums but turned down the chance to star in the Broadway show *South Pacific*, due to a lack of confidence. This was not helped by autograph hunters scrambling for Zsa Zsa's signature and not his. The actress was no shrinking violet, as his previous wife had been. The more sarcastic and dismissive Sanders was of Zsa Zsa and her career, the more hurt she felt. Their different film roles kept them apart, often for long periods, and George delighted in telling his wife of his infidelities. It was while she was filming in France that Zsa Zsa succumbed to the flattering attentions of the Dominican Ambassador to France. By the end of 1953, the Sanders' marriage was over and they were divorced in April 1954.

The split did nothing to help George's troubled and insecure mind; he had been in psychotherapy since his first wife had walked out on him in 1946. Now, he hid behind a mask of haughtiness and superciliousness, becoming reclusive and avoiding social situations as far as possible, even falling asleep on set, between takes, in order not to have to make conversation. Still searching for the pot of gold that would give him the financial security and cultural freedom he craved, Sanders channelled his energies into setting up a company with two research and development engineers. George made himself managing director and set about designing an impressive office and selling stock to his friends. His two research buddies faded into the background but kept their hands in the till. When his friend and fellow actor, Brian Aherne, turned up at the factory to check on his investment, he found the premises had been picked clean and deserted. All enquiries, the caretaker informed Aherne, should be referred to Sanders's lawyer. The company was in receivership and George's house and car had been seized and his bank accounts frozen. Sanders fled to Spain to make a film and renounced his American residency in order to protect himself from creditors, including friends to whom he'd sold stock. Next stop was Japan, to make another film. If Plan 'A' didn't work for George, there was always Plan 'B'.

Marrying money wasn't the easy task Sanders thought it would be. After several amorous interludes with wealthy ladies, George had not calculated on falling in love with an old friend. In 1959, he married Ronald Colman's widow, the former actress Benita Hume. He had known Benita in Hollywood for nearly twenty years; she was as English in spirit as he was and he had no need to hide behind any mask with her. Their marriage was a blissfully happy one, or it should have been. The couple set about finding a tax haven so that George could keep most of his earnings and they could live in a style to which Sanders wished to become accustomed. They settled on the city of Lausanne in Switzerland and joined the circle of ex-pats that Benita called 'The Alpine Set': Niv and Noël,

Burton and Brynner, Chaplin and countless others. These were blessed days. George set to work to make money, taking almost any film part, and Benita was the adoring, but never boring, wife who soothed his fevered brow at the end of the day. They had a comfortable home, with servants and a secretary, and George was fond of his step-daughter, Juliet Colman. But Sanders couldn't resist having another shot at business tycoonery. It was his tragedian flaw, and it would make his last years with Benita doubly tragic.

James Mason was doing well in Hollywood in the 1950's, if not by his own artistic standards. He had come to realise, like his friend George Sanders, that work was the thing, and to hell with intellectual ideals. And he had landed one or two interesting roles in films such as *The Desert Fox, A Star is Born* with Judy Garland, and *North By Northwest* with Cary Grant. But, instead of capitalising on his successes, he chose to return to theatre work, this time in Canada, much to the annoyance of his wife who had worked so hard to further his film career. For James, it was a welcome break from California. He had never felt at ease there, as his wife had done, but he now had a son, Morgan, as well as his daughter, Portland, and he was trying hard to ignore his yearning to return to Europe and its culture. Yet he couldn't hide his frustration with his work and the Hollywood press. He tried his hand at producing a film, which proved popular only in Europe. He was as withdrawn at home as he was on film sets and his marriage began to suffer.

Mason hated the Californian sunshine and palm trees and the whole Hollywood construct. He had an affair with a publicist from Chicago, which didn't help his marriage, and filmed on location in Scotland and revisited his home in Yorkshire, which didn't help his longing for Europe. George Sanders was also on location with James in Scotland for the film *A Touch of Larceny*. George had now found happiness with Benita Hume, and James formed a romantic attachment to the lead actress, Vera Miles. Perhaps observing George's domestic happiness prompted Mason to sort out his own life. He could see the movie industry was becoming more international now and less dependent on an American base as the studio system folded. He returned to his family in Hollywood but continued to seek solace in his affair with the Chicago publicist. He was torn between two worlds and the stress of it all brought him out in a nervous rash. He loved books and music and Europe, but he also loved his children. Then, in 1962, came the role of Humbert Humbert in *Lolita*, which was shot by Stanley Kubrick in England. The film not only put James back on the professional map but he knew he'd come home, geographically.

George Sanders was delighted to be back in Europe in 1960. Everything was perfect: his marriage was wonderful in every way, his film work was regular and remunerative, and his new business scheme for manufacturing sausages was keeping him and his two partners, Thomas Roe and Denis Loraine, busy. His friends in the film industry were happy to invest in the Royal Victorian Sausage Company and Roe and Loraine drew in more famous and wealthy clients. No expense was spared on the business side and George and Benita enjoyed travelling and seeing their friends in Europe and the States. It wasn't until 1964 that dark clouds began to gather in their blue-sky existence. The sausage company started to run out of money and still hadn't manufactured a single sausage and, worst of all, Benita was found to have breast cancer and needed urgent surgery.

When Thomas Roe and Denis Loraine were arrested for fraud in 1965, it was time for George and Benita to leave Switzerland. They went, first of all, back to the States where George landed a plum part in a musical. But the production, and George in particular, was savaged by the critics. More devastating to Sanders was being told that his beloved wife had only months to live. They planned to buy a cheap house back in Europe, in Mallorca, and George went to Spain to complete the purchase while Benita, now weak and in pain was flown to England. George was at her bedside at the end, desperate to help her in her agony. They had made a pact to help one another, if necessary, avoid a painful death. But poor Benita could not swallow without being sick and George had to watch, helplessly, as Benita's life ebbed away. He never got over losing her. The haughty, sneering mask was put back firmly in place.

Fortunately, by the time James Mason moved to Switzerland in 1962, he had absolutely no money to invest in the grandiose schemes being hatched by Sanders and co. in Lausanne. He was flat broke after his divorce from Pamela but happy to be free and back in Europe. He had asked for the divorce and allowed himself to be sued for adultery. Now, after the success of *Lolita*, he hoped to keep some of his earnings after paying maintenance to his ex-wife, but he knew that would not be possible if he returned to Britain with its high rate of income tax. He needed a low tax country in Europe with high speed connections to film locations in any part of the world.

Others, such as Richard Burton, Audrey Hepburn, David Niven, Noël Coward, Charlie Chaplin, Yul Brynner, William Holden, Deborah Kerr and his old friend George Sanders had shown the way. But Pamela had taken him to the cleaners and, although James took every reasonable film offer he could, he arrived in Switzerland only able to afford two rooms on the ground floor of his bank manager's chalet in Vevey, with a packing crate to sit on.

As Peter Ustinov would do after his Swiss divorce, Mason took every type of job on offer. Like Ustinov, he made commercials for TV and took parts in films that would not be memorable except for his classy presence. Then came a string of hits: *The Blue Max, Georgy Girl*, for which he received an Oscar nomination, and *The Deadly Affair*, a John Le Carré story directed by Sidney Lumet. But he appeared sad and lost at this time, lonely but afraid of committing himself to another marriage, although he was pursued by some glamorous women, including his neighbour, the Countess Crespi. He was leading an unfulfilled life, both artistically and personally, wandering the globe making forgettable films to pay the bills. He bought a small house in Corseaux, a village on Lake Geneva just outside Vevey, and spent his spare time sketching and walking in the hillside vineyards with his visiting children. Soon after, he was reunited with Clarissa Kaye, an actress with whom he had shared a bed scene in a film shot in Australia. The two had kept in touch and, when Clarissa won some money on the horses and took herself off on a world cruise, she dropped in on James in Switzerland and stayed with him until his death, fourteen years later. They married, in a low-key ceremony in Corseaux, in August 1971.

George Sanders had lost the one woman who had brought stability to his life and made everything he did worthwhile. Now Benita was gone and so was the money he'd accumulated. His film career consisted of mediocre parts in second-class films. He led a rudderless existence and his health, which had always been robust, was beginning to fail him. He remained friends with Zsa Zsa Gabor, who continued to have a soft spot for George, the third of her nine husbands. After Benita died in 1968, he held on to the little house in Mallorca, though he would never have left Switzerland if it hadn't been for the sausage scandal. He had been supremely happy there.

Zsa Zsa was concerned about Sanders; he was depressed and had suffered several strokes, his speech was slurred and he was partially deaf in one ear. He also suffered from vertigo and often fell over, injuring himself. Because of his health problems, work was drying up. He asked Zsa Zsa to marry him again. Ever practical, Zsa Zsa decided to inject a little happiness into his life. In December 1970, she arranged for George to marry her wealthy sister, Magda, who had also suffered a debilitating stroke. Sanders went along with it; Magda was an old friend. The marriage lasted all of six weeks and was annulled in mid-January 1971.

After his strokes, Sanders had been told to lay off the sauce, which he sensibly did, hoping to improve his health and work again. But, after his divorce from Magda, he met a woman who liked to drink. He joined in the fun and left Europe for Los Angeles to be with his ladyfriend. She suggested he sell his home in Mallorca; his judgement clouded, George did just that. He immediately regretted losing the haven he had bought for Benita and himself and, feeling lost in the world, Sanders had a nervous breakdown.

He was now downing straight vodkas, popping pills and looking pale and ill. Zsa Zsa Gabor saw George in London on 20 April 1972 and was concerned about him. He had been to visit his sister in Sussex and talked of buying a beach house near Barcelona. On 23 April, Sanders arrived at Barcelona airport and spoke to the group of reporters who surrounded him there. He checked into a hotel suite and continued drinking steadily. He asked for an early morning call. The next morning, when he didn't answer his wake-up call, the manager went to his room. George had written a short note, swallowed around sixty capsules of barbiturates and a large amount of vodka and had lain down to die. In his note he explained that he was bored with the world and that was why he was leaving it. It was a front, a mask, a continuation of his screen persona. He was, in fact, lost and unhappy and saw no future for himself except poverty and ill-health. All his life, he had wanted security and he had ended up with nothing at all. He couldn't bear it. George was cremated and his ashes were scattered in the English Channel. He had always loved the sea.

The second Mrs James Mason had a personality quite as strong as the first one. James seemed to prefer his women that way. But Clarissa Kaye, twenty-five years younger than her husband, brought a stability to his life and a healthier lifestyle than he had been leading. She worried continually about his health; James had already had one heart attack and, now, the doctor in Vevey recommended that he have a pacemaker fitted. In the 1970's, Mason was finally recognised as a first-class character actor, an elder statesman type of figure in films. Work was steady, he was in constant demand and Clarissa was not only always by his side but often playing roles in his films. Like George Sanders, James was often a supporting actor, rather than the star of a film, but he was making money and, unlike old George, holding on to it. He worked with his neighbour, Audrey Hepburn, on *Bloodline* but the actress was having problems with her personal life and the production was not a happy one. He enjoyed working with another neighbour, Roger Moore, on the thriller *North Sea Hijack* and with another Swiss resident, Peter Ustinov, in an Agatha Christie-Hercule Poirot film. But it was his memorable role in *The Verdict* with Paul Newman that won him a further Oscar nomination. In spite of his failing health, he still couldn't bring himself to turn down work, always worrying about money.

Fitted with the pacemaker, James pushed himself on, making the film *Alexandre* for Swiss TV. Then came the offer of a BBC film of Graham Greene's novella *Doctor Fischer of Geneva and the Bomb Party*, which Mason could hardly refuse. Filmed on location in the snow on the shores of Lake Geneva in deepest winter, James did his professional best and gave a first class performance. Clarissa, who also had a part in the film, knew how ill he was and kept a close eye on him. When an offer came to take over Paul Schofield's role in *The Shooting Party*, she understood why her husband couldn't turn the part down, even though it meant filming without a break after *Dr Fischer*.

James was exhausted by the time he and Clarissa returned to Corseaux. He intended to recuperate in

Switzerland while looking at yet more film scripts. One warm evening in July, Mason felt ill and Clarissa cancelled their dinner date. That night, he woke with a dreadful pain in his back and was rushed to the hospital in Lausanne. The end came quickly: Mason died of heart failure on 27 July 1984 at the age of seventy-five.

Unlike the remains of his friend, George Sanders, James Mason's ashes were not scattered or buried, or anything else. Instead, they resided in an urn on his widow's mantelpiece while Clarissa and James's children, Portland and Morgan, were locked in a long legal battle over Mason's will. The actor, thanks to Swiss taxes, had amassed a fortune worth millions of pounds by the time he died. He left his children a hand-written note, asking them to exercise patience; he had left everything to Clarissa, believing she had sacrificed her acting career for his. He may have presumed she would pass the estate on to Portland and Morgan, but his friends believed Clarissa disliked her husband's children. Alone in Corseaux and failing in health, Clarissa became involved with a religious sect. When she died of cancer in 1994, the children traced James's ashes to a bank deposit box. But it was to be another five years before a court would allow them to scatter their father's ashes over his headstone in the cemetery at Corsier-sur-Vevey, just yards from where his old friend, Charlie Chaplin, lay. Only months after the ceremony, Mason's daughter, Portland, had a major stroke. She died, tragically young, at the age of fifty-five, while writing a book about her father, leaving Morgan to continue the fight for his father's possessions and memorabilia.

Mason had thought at various times that his children would follow him into acting but, in the end, although both had parts in several films, they pursued other careers. James did balk at a suggestion that his daughter play the title role in Stanley Kubrick's film version of Vladimir Nabokov's novel *Lolita*, and the part of the nymphet went to Sue Lyon. Nabokov and Mason would be neighbours and friends throughout the Sixties and most of the Seventies when Vladimir, like James, moved to Switzerland from America. But, unlike James, Nabokov lived in some luxury in the splendid Montreux Palace Hotel, just a few kilometres along the lake from Mason's village home.

Chapter 5
Vladimir Nabokov

'V'ladimir, love of my life, father of my son. *Mon amour, ma raison d'être.* Vlah-dee-meer: the teeth tap the lower lip on one, the tongue hits the palate, two, and the mouth compresses, briefly, on three. Vlah. Dee. Meer.

You were Lody, simply Lody, the rich and gifted child of a Russian politician, catching butterflies in the summer sunshine. You were Sirin, the handsome poet, setting hearts a-flutter in Berlin when they killed your father. You were Vladimir Vladimirovich Nabokov to officialdom as we fled Paris and Hitler's tanks and begged tickets for the *Champlain*'s last Atlantic voyage. You were Professor Nabokov the eccentric, lecturing on American campuses, purveyor of pornography, they said, when *Lolita*'s tragic tale was told. In Switzerland, you were a global business: VN, the world-famous writer. But in my thoughts and dreams you will always be Volodya, roaming the mountains with your butterfly net, searching, constantly searching for perfection in nature's art ... '

Véra Nabokov smiled wistfully as she stood on the balcony of the suite of rooms at the top of the Montreux Palace Hotel. The slim, elegant, white-haired lady looked frailer than usual that evening and her eyes were rheumy. She gazed across the lake at the majestic Dents du Midi, its snow-capped rocks on fire in the blood-red sunset. Her thin fingers clutched the balcony rail and she glanced down at the chattering tourists in the busy Grand Rue. Something caught her eye, or had she imagined it? Was that a butterfly dancing in the half-light? At this hour? In this season? She watched the winged form flutter towards the tops of the trees on the other side of the crowded street: traffic horns, people shouting and laughing, tables outside cafés and music within. Véra sighed and stepped back carefully into the *belle époque* room. Slowly, she closed one tall french window after the other and fumbled with the old-fashioned catch, then she turned and, with faltering steps, disappeared into the darkened room, away from the dying light.

Vladimir Vladimirovich Nabokov, poet, author, playwright, screenwriter, artist, boxer, footballer, tennis coach, academic and lepidopterist, was born in St

Petersburg, Russia, on 23 April 1899. His parents were a wealthy, loving, educated couple; part of the Russian intelligentsia of the period and closely connected to royalty and the government of the day. The Nabokovs' first child was still-born and when, a year later, Vladimir arrived, he was immediately the adored centre of his parents' world. This situation did not change when his brother, Sergei, was born a year later, or his two sisters and brother, after that. Lody, as Vladimir was called, a shortened version of the pet name Volodya, not only had a privileged upbringing but a very happy one. His father was a prominent liberal politician, lawyer, scholar, sportsman and avid collector of butterflies while his mother, attractive and wealthy, was a gifted artist who brought to the marriage the beautiful country estate of Vyra where the family spent carefree, idyllic summers and where Vladimir began to share his father's passion for lepidoptery, butterfly collecting.

The Nabokov children were brought up to be tri-lingual. They found French and English easy to use, plus Latin for their school books, but they had to be coached in Russian: a language used by ordinary folk and the children's servants. The family lived in a large town house in St Petersburg with an enormous library of ten thousand books. Both parents delighted in reading to their children whenever they could. The library was also where Vladimir's father worked when he was at home and where he installed a punch-bag and taught young Lody to box. His mother encouraged the boy's artistic side and his recall for detail, so that, later on, Nabokov would think of particular words in terms of colours and use vibrant imagery in his writing. Sergei was the musical child in the family but he was also timid and unsure of himself. Vladimir had no time for his brother's lack of confidence and would prefer to play with his older cousin than the effeminate Sergei. It was only when Nabokov came across Sergei's diary, one day, that he realised why his brother was in psychological turmoil. Sergei knew he was homosexual from a young age, and the very different interests of the two brothers would prevent them being close, even though they would go through harsh and dangerous times together.

The ubiquitous George Sanders, future Hollywood matinée idol and much else besides, was also born into a privileged household in cultural St Petersburg, in 1906. Like Lody, young George was loved by his parents, given the best of educations and enjoyed carefree summers on the large family estates. But Mr Sanders has intruded in several lives already and we must grasp him firmly by the lapels of his cashmere coat and eject him from this account. It will not be our fault if he reappears, now and then, when we consider Vladimir Nabokov's interest in art, sport, women, money-making, books, the film world and Switzerland. Both of these 'White Russians', as the ex-ruling class were called after the Bolshevik revolution in 1917, were obliged to begin their lives again, several times over. We can only speculate on why the paths of two such tall, handsome, articulate men diverged so spectacularly.

By the time Nabokov was born at the end of the nineteenth century, the old social order in Russia, with its tsars, serfs and rigid system of exclusion and privilege, was moving slowly in a more enlightened direction. Too slowly. Those who could have modified laws and prevented discontent growing amongst the oppressed, lacked the vision or power, or both, to do so. A few thinkers and liberal politicians demanded reform, especially after the Bloody Sunday massacre of 1905 when fleeing children attempted to hide in trees after a peaceful demonstration and were shot at by troops. But the progressives' speeches and pamphlets went unheeded or landed them in prison. Vladimir's father would be arrested on more than one occasion and his name was second on a hit list of former politicians after the dissolution of the first Russian parliament. The first name on the list was assassinated. After that, Nabokov's parents left Russia and stayed in Europe for a while. When they returned, Vladimir's father and fellow liberal politicians had to stand trial for signing a manifesto against the power of the tsar. Three months of solitary confinement in prison followed. His father wrote from his cell to Vladimir about butterflies, the passion they shared. When Nabokov senior was released, the children continued to be privately tutored and taken to school in chauffeur-driven limousines, but it was a period of easy living that was about to end.

At school, one day, Vladimir learned from his playground chums that his father, who was now the editor of a liberal newspaper, had been obliged to 'call out' a writer on the staff of a conservative paper whom he had accused of taking huge bribes from the suppliers of the city's trams. The writer had responded to the accusation by declaring that Nabokov's father had only married his wife for her money, and the insulted editor had no choice but to challenge the man to a duel. All day at school, Vladimir worried about the outcome of the event. He imagined returning to the house, only to be told that his father was dead. The schoolboy rushed home that afternoon, full of emotion, and fell into the hallway where he could hear adult voices. They were discussing how the other party in the disagreement had apologised at the last moment, as they had known he would. Vladimir could not control his tearful sobs of relief. Far away, in South America, however, a few years later, Casanova George Sanders would be challenged to a duel by a cuckolded fiancé. The result of that encounter would be quite different: near-death for one of the duellists and deportation for the other.

To the lush summer estate at Vyra, where the Nabokov children gambolled and chased butterflies, read books and painted in the sunshine, was added another vast property. One of Vladimir's uncles died tragically young of heart failure and, having no heirs, left a vast acreage of land and property worth millions to the seventeen year-old boy. Vladimir used the building for trysts with a young girl who was holidaying in the region. He was always interested in the opposite sex and would conduct several affairs at once which, in turn, would inspire him to write books of poetry, as well as short stories and novels.

But this paradise was about to be lost. The First World War (1914-1918) saw Russian troops fighting under appalling conditions which only served to fan the flames of discontent amongst their families back home. Now, every class of Russian, rich and poor, could see social unrest was coming. Food was in short supply and hundreds of thousands of workers went on strike and demonstrated in St Petersburg. Troops refused to obey orders to suppress the gatherings this time. Instead, arms depots were broken into and guns and rifles handed around. Shooting and carnage followed. The tsar was forced to abdicate. The Russian Revolution was on.

Nabokov's father held a post in the provisional government that followed the tsar's removal but the administration could not legislate for reform fast enough to satisfy those who had been oppressed. An agitator called Lenin seized the moment and returned from exile in Switzerland to orchestrate the changing situation. Law and order broke down and the government was forced to resign. With shooting in the streets, the Nabokov family left the city to spend summer on their estate at Vyra, as usual. In the autumn of 1917, they returned to St Petersburg, just as the Bolsheviks seized power. Although he admired his father's principles, Vladimir was not politically-minded, himself. He took refuge in his poetry and hobbies during the unrest and, when the family home was broken into by armed men, he was found practising his boxing skills on his father's punch-ball in the library, and nearly mistaken for a Cossack in hiding.

Immediately, his father made plans to evacuate the family. First, Vladimir and his brother, Sergei, were put on a train to the estate of a friend in the Crimea. During the journey, the train was boarded by frustrated soldiers returning from the front and intent on mischief. The two Nabokovs locked themselves in their carriage while the soldiers urinated down the vents. When the carriage door was finally kicked open, Sergei pretended he had an acute case of typhoid and the brothers were able to continue their journey without further harassment.

Soon, Nabokov's mother and sisters and youngest brother joined them on the estate near Yalta. The family had not been able to bring anything of value with them except a few jewels hidden in a container of talcum powder. Back in St Petersburg, Vladimir's father was arrested by the Bolsheviks and held for five days. He was released but, on learning he was about to be rearrested, headed straight for his family in the Crimea without returning home. He was luckier than some of his colleagues, who were killed while under arrest. The family was followed to Yalta by their former valet, who brought them some money. By now, there were many refugee families like the Nabokovs, short of food and living a low-key existence in order not to attract attention to themselves while the Bolsheviks, followed by the Germans, took control of the region. There was nothing they could do but wait out the conflict. As George Sanders observed when his own family lost everything and fled to Europe, almost all White Russians believed the situation was a temporary one. Prague, Paris and Berlin would become popular centres in which the displaced wealthy lived in genteel poverty while they waited for their country to be restored to them. Vladimir occupied himself with his passion for collecting butterflies, as well as meeting a number of attractive young girls.

When the Germans retreated from the Crimea in 1919 and the Communists took over, it was time for the White Russians to flee once more. By April, there was only one escape route: the port of Sebastopol. Refugees filled the streets, sleeping on their suitcases in the squares at night. The Nabokovs were lucky; Vladimir's father, as a former government minister, was given rooms at a hotel. It was the height of luxury compared to what was to come. A boat was found for the ex-ministers and their families.

It had been fire-damaged and was not much more than burned timbers, but it would save them from the clutches of the approaching Red Army. Or would it?

The French would not allow the ministers and their families to leave unless all ex-government funds were handed over to them. The Nabokovs watched the boat set sail for Constantinople without them. Negotiations led to another boat being found: a foul little cargo ship with one rough cabin for seven ministers and their wives and children. In total, thirty-five people were obliged to sleep on wooden benches in the dirty cabin during the three days the boat remained in port. When the vessel was finally allowed to leave harbour, Vladimir and his father preferred to remain on deck, playing a game of chess, rather than stay in the cramped quarters below, in spite of a hail of machine-gun bullets whizzing over their heads from the shore-line. They had no idea they were seeing their beloved country for the last time, and they had little idea what moves they would be obliged to make in the future.

Meanwhile, a beautiful but fragile Jewish girl and her family were also fleeing the Bolsheviks. The Slonims' circuitous and dangerous journey from St Petersburg would bring them, finally, to Yalta one year after Vladimir and his family had left Russia forever. Véra was just eighteen years old and weakened by the family's trek to the Crimea, the last outpost of White Russia. Her father, Evsei Slonim managed to get his family on a boat headed for Istanbul. Slonim was an intelligent and previously successful businessman who'd had the foresight to transfer his funds out of Russia via a Dutch business partner. The family's difficult journey from Istanbul to

Sofia then took them on to Vienna, a city which seemed full of luxury after the harsh conditions they had experienced and where food was gloriously abundant, something the Slonims had not known for three years. Rested, the family pushed on to Germany, a country that was tolerant of political refugees at the time. In Berlin, Evsei Slonim went into business, once again. He sent one of his three daughters to the Sorbonne in Paris and another to a boarding school near Lausanne, in Switzerland. The third one, the good-looking Véra, had been a sickly child with breathing problems and was still unwell after all their upheavals. Although she was intelligent, Evsei did not put her into higher education, believing that study would weaken her further. Instead, Véra took a stenographer's course and went to work for her father in his import-export business. She was a fast learner and soon became an astute businesswoman, an excellent multi-tasker and an extremely hard-working one. Lucky Vladimir Nabokov.

The french windows opened slowly and the white-haired woman stepped gingerly onto the balcony. She held the wrought-iron rail and peered down at the evening promenaders strolling along the lakeside paths: the families, the couples arm-in-arm. A butterfly danced close by, on a current of warm air, so delicate-looking against the backdrop of the Haute Savoie mountains. Véra smiled as she remembered those mountain trips her husband had made, searching for Coppers and Blues, Swallowtails and Fritillaries, in a landscape that reminded him of the cloudless days of his boyhood. It was not the first time she had noticed butterflies hovering above the balcony where they had played chess together so often. And now ...

'Volodya, my husband ... ' Véra's voice wavered a little, perhaps with emotion, or because of her age. She cleared her throat and began again, whispering his name this time. She had spent the afternoon answering questions from a journalist who had wanted to know how Véra Slonim had met the celebrated poet Vladimir Sirin in Weimar Berlin in the decadent 1920's. The story was a romantic one: masked balls and trysts and love letters, the reporter reminded her. But he'd done some checking, he said. Dates, events, they didn't tally. Véra was tired. Tired of reporters now. She'd had decades of facing the press with Vladimir. He'd hated giving interviews without her. She regarded the butterfly again, darting to and fro in front of her, then she gave a small, almost imperceptible chuckle. 'Details, Lody ... You were always one for detail in your stories. How do they know what really happened? Were they there?' The butterfly appeared to hover above her and she glimpsed its mother-of-pearl underside. Then she watched it flit, almost skip, gaily away.

The Nabokovs reached the port of Constantinople in Turkey on 16 April 1919. The small amount of food they had brought with them was already finished and they waited to go ashore. And waited. Constantinople was already overrun with refugees and the Nabokovs and their fellow passengers were refused permission to land. The families waited on the dirty vessel for another two days before it moved off, bound for the port of Piraeus in Athens, Greece. In spite of the fact they had used up all their water, they had to spend another two days in quarantine aboard the cargo boat. When the families were finally allowed on shore, they fled the industrial docks and found themselves two clean and decent hotels. They were desperately short of money now, but they had their standards. For three and a half weeks they took in classical sights, such as the Acropolis, while they planned their next move. Vladimir wrote poetry and busied himself searching for butterflies and young ladies. He managed three love affairs during their short stay.

The ship that carried the Nabokovs onwards to France was a far classier affair. Their money was running out fast but the family sailed to Marseilles in style on a Cunard liner. Clean and spacious and boasting its own floating art gallery, the young Vladimir learned to dance in the grand ballroom; there were no butterflies to distract him on the voyage. From Marseilles, the family caught the train to Paris where Vladimir elected to go with a young woman friend to sell his mother's pearls to Cartier, the jeweller. Dishevelled after his long journey, the shop staff were convinced the young man was a thief and called the police. Vladimir only managed to convince them he was a refugee minutes before the gendarmes arrived.

Three days later, the Nabokovs took the cross-channel boat to Southampton, England, and headed straight for London where they had arranged to meet Vladimir's uncle at Victoria Station. But, delighted as his uncle was to see them, he was unable to help Vladimir's father find work, even though he, himself, had held a post at the Russian Embassy in London before the revolution. The family lodged in expensive rooms in South Kensington before moving to a house in Elm Park Gardens, close to where Peter Ustinov would spend his childhood. London, liked Paris and Berlin, was full of Russian refugees in 1919. The Nabokovs existed on money they received for the jewels they had smuggled out of Russia. The situation was still seen as temporary; they would all go home to St Petersburg soon. Vladimir resumed his romancing and ballroom dancing, as well as a spot of tennis on the London courts with Sergei.

In the autumn, the two brothers went up to university, as had been arranged before leaving Russia. Sergei went to Oxford and Vladimir to Cambridge. Vladimir was a keen sportsman and shone on the football pitch and the tennis court, and even took part in boxing tournaments. But, cultured and urbane though Vladimir was, he always felt, like his future friend and neighbour, Peter Ustinov, an outsider in English society. His friends remained Russian, for the most part. The English, at this time, saw the Russian revolution as the liberation of an oppressed people. It would be half a century before they would learn of the violence and atrocities that were taking place. Nabokov had intended to study zoology but, after a couple of terms of dissecting fish and other foul-smelling specimens, he switched to French and Russian and decided to concentrate on a literary career and become a first-class Russian writer. He not only absorbed all he could of Russian and French literature but also immersed himself in English poetry. Always an insomniac, he would sit up in bed at night, smoking one Turkish cigarette after another and writing furiously in Russian.

But Vladimir was homesick. He missed his boyhood homes, not because of the material wealth that had surrounded him but because of the love and happiness and laughter he had known in those carefree days. George

Sanders had also arrived in England with his brother and had been sent to a college in Brighton which he found contrasted harshly to his pampered childhood in St Petersburg. Like the Nabokovs, the Sanders family was existing on the proceeds of jewellery sales, as well as the generosity of a relative who had fled to Switzerland. George also missed those balmy summer days on the family estates and the good life in St Petersburg. But, unlike Vladimir Nabokov, George deeply regretted the loss of his family's wealth. He maintained he was born to be indolent, a state of being which required a great deal of money.

In 1920, Vladimir's father decided to move his family to Berlin where he was to edit a Russian newspaper. Vladimir, who had tried to get summer jobs while at university, was happy to submit pieces to the newspaper, using the pen name Vladimir Sirin, so as not to be confused with his father, Vladimir D. Nabokov. Sirin, in Russian folklore, was the name for a bird of paradise and the writer would use the name in a variety of spellings over the next two decades. He continued to work hard for his final exams, which he passed with distinction, and enjoyed love affairs, often with several women at once. In the holidays, he joined his family in Berlin where a respectable Russian émigré society was forming. And a respected Russian writer was what Vladimir Nabokov wanted to be.

Vladimir's poetry was published in book form, as well as in journals, and he was experimenting with writing plays. The Nabokovs were at the centre of Russian cultural life in the city and the family home, particularly at the table, was a meeting point for intellectual exchanges and debate. Life was going forward again, or so it seemed. Vladimir's mother was working hard raising funds for the famine in Russia, while her husband continued his political activities in readiness for the family's return to their beloved country. One evening, on 28 March 1922, while Vladimir was over from England for the Easter holiday, his father attended a political meeting and shared the platform with a former Russian minister who had been invited to speak about the restoration of Russia. The meeting was well-attended: around fifteen hundred Russians crowded into the hall to hear the speech. Suddenly, two anti-monarchists broke from the crowd and rushed at the platform with guns, intending to assassinate the speaker. Vladimir's father and a colleague pinned the first gunman to the ground, but the second assassin shot Nabokov senior three times and killed him almost instantly. Vladimir and his mother were sitting at home, reading and discussing poetry, when the telephone call came through that would change their lives.

If his father's death demolished his mother, it pushed Vladimir even more strongly in the direction of building a writing career. But, unusually for Nabokov, he was depressed, and proposed to a seventeen year-old girl called Svetlana whose parents insisted the poet find a steady job if he wanted to marry their daughter. Both Vladimir and Sergei were given posts in a bank. Sergei held down his post for a whole week; Vladimir could only manage three hours' employment. He preferred to get by doing translation work or compiling chess problems for a newspaper, or tutoring in French and English and giving tennis and boxing lessons. He needed to be free to compose if he were to become a famous writer. He tried to enter the film world and worked as an extra, although he would never become a screen idol like that other square-jawed Russian from St Petersburg, George Sanders.

Life was cheap in Berlin in 1923 and full of Russian publishing houses. Vladimir published four books of poetry in four months and as Sirin, the tall and handsome poet celebrated for his public readings, he made many a young lady's heart flutter in his audiences. Véra Slonim began to attend these readings and she collected press cuttings about the poet. Meanwhile, Svetlana's parents were not impressed by Vladimir's writerly activities and forced their daughter to break off her engagement to him. In just over six months, Vladimir had lost both his adored father and his fiancée. He was emotionally distraught and immersed himself in his writing. He decided to take off for the South of France to do some fruit picking on the farm of a family friend. The change, he felt would do him good and he could enjoy collecting butterflies again. He just had time to attend one of the many Russian charity balls held in Berlin at that time, before leaving for Toulon. There, he encountered a mysterious woman in a wolf mask. He was captivated by her conversation and attracted by her elegant bearing. He followed her outside, sensing he had met his destiny. As soon as Nabokov returned from the South of France, he and Véra Slonim were reunited. From that moment, they formed the partnership of a lifetime.

Vladimir's mother moved to Prague, taking her youngest children with her. German inflation was eating into incomes and many Russians left for Paris or Prague, including most of the Russian publishing houses. Books were pulped by the thousands, but Vladimir stayed on and continued to write. He took whatever jobs he could, teaching, articles, as long as they didn't interfere with his work. Véra was already translating and typing his writing for him, as she would do for the next five decades. The couple married on 15 April 1925, but had little money for the ceremony with two anonymous witnesses. Yet, with Véra's support, Nabokov's writing acquired a new force and compression. Their circle of friends became a literary one and Vladimir's public readings brought him to the notice of the right people, even if there was little money to be made from the events. Véra's father had lost his business, but she found work in other offices. Vladimir was now producing novels and making some money from the serial rights. They took a holiday in the South of France where Véra learned to catch butterflies. They took out a loan on a small plot of land and Nabokov hoped they could live on his writing but, by 1929, money was tight again; there were not enough Russians left in Berlin for him to write for and the Wall Street crash heralded economic depression and the start of political upheaval.

By 1932, Blackshirts and Brownshirts were prowling the streets of Berlin and Hitler was soon to become Chancellor. The Nabokovs had to give up their small plot of land and often had no money to send to Vladimir's mother, who was now living in abject poverty in Prague. Vladimir went to Paris, the new Russian émigré centre, to give public readings of his work and to make himself known to French publishers. He also met up with old friends and relatives, including Sergei, who was now living in the city. But Nabokov was so short of money that he had to borrow clothes in order to be decently attired for his readings. Would Paris be his future? He wanted it to be. In Berlin, they were burning books, not printing them, and Véra, being Jewish, was having difficulty finding work. But a momentous event was about to occur that would change the Nabokovs' lives: Véra was expecting a child; the move to France was put on hold.

Dmitri Nabokov was born in May 1934, in the dark days of the rise to power of the Nazi party. But to Vladimir and Véra, their son was a breath of spring air and the baby was adored by his parents quite as much as Volodya had been cherished as a child in Russia. Berlin was not an easy place for Nabokov to earn money and Véra was driven to the point of exhaustion, caring for Dmitri and taking dictation from Vladimir and typing up his work. They both believed in his writing talent. Literary agents in America, as well as in Europe, were trying to sell his work. But Vladimir discovered, when he read some of his writing in translation, that terrible mistakes had been made in the texts. He decided he would translate his work himself, whenever he or Véra could. It was one of the deciding factors that would lead him to become such a skilled writer in English, although Nabokov was unhappy with his first efforts in the language.

Another successful reading tour in Paris and Belgium made France an attractive alternative to living in Germany. When, in May 1936, the man who had shot and killed his father was elected Deputy Head of Hitler's right-wing department for immigration, Vladimir knew it was time for them to leave the country. He applied for jobs in the United States and in England, but could not find decent employment in either country. There was nothing for it; Nabokov set off for another reading tour of France, England and Belgium. He left behind his wife and their big, boisterous son. He was never to return Germany. His life was entering a new phase. And the name of the woman who was to upset the Nabokovs' perfect marriage was Irina.

She was as beautiful as Véra, and as cultured, and she had a mother who was determined that Monsieur Sirinne would be her son-in-law. Both mother and daughter had attended one of Vladimir's readings in Paris, where they lived among the large Russian émigré population. When Irina's mother realised her daughter was smitten by the writer, she went to work, inviting Nabokov to literary gatherings and dinners with the young woman. Vladimir grew close to Irina and was soon in love with her. What could he do? He had the best of wives in Véra and a beloved son whom he adored. Yet, he could not give up Irina. It was a situation he never thought he would find himself in, it was tearing him apart. He could only hope the affair would burn itself out. But Irina would not allow that.

Nabokov continued to make plans for his family to join him in France. He obtained the necessary *carte de séjour* while Véra packed up their apartment in Berlin. They agreed to meet in Prague where Véra took Dmitri so that Vladimir's mother might see her grandson. Someone was not happy with the Nabokovs' plans and wrote an anonymous letter to Véra, giving a detailed account of her husband's affair. Was it Irina's mother, or Irina herself? Vladimir insisted to his wife that he loved only her but, still, he could not break with Irina and wrote to her secretly. He returned to Paris with Véra and Dmitri and saw Irina several times. The Nabokovs moved south to Cannes. The marriage was under a terrible strain. Véra told her husband to go to his mistress. Vladimir demurred. Irina said she would come to Cannes and they could leave together. Still Nabokov delayed in making a decision. Finally, Irina travelled south to confront her lover. She found the address of his apartment and waited on the nearby beach for Vladimir to come down to the sea with his son. Nabokov was horrified when he saw his mistress and asked her to leave. But she wouldn't. She sat down on the sand, close by, and watched as Véra joined her husband and son. She remained on the beach when the family went back for lunch and Vladimir never saw her again. The Nabokovs repaired their marriage and focussed on Dmitri and turning Volodya into a world-class writer. Vladimir was now looking west, to New York and Hollywood films. He knew he would have to give up writing in Russian, once and for all, and become an English writer.

It was 1938 and everyone knew war was coming. Nabokov still hoped to get a job in England or America, but his books were not selling well there. The family was continually short of money, although they ate well and made sure Dmitri had the best quality food. Vladimir asked the Russian Literary Fund in America for some money. He was desperate, but they could only send him twenty dollars. His future neighbour in Switzerland, Noël Coward, was the highest paid writer in the world at this time. It was one of Coward's plays that took George Sanders to Broadway. Soon, George was on his way to Hollywood where he was regularly cast as a villain. Sanders did not object; he soon found acting the cad brought in the money. But he realised that acting success lay in the quality of the part created by the writer.

Back in Paris in 1939, Nabokov turned his attention to writing for the theatre but his play was cancelled before it was staged. He began to write his first novel in English but he was not happy with his command of the language. He felt he needed to live in an English-speaking environment to break into the English-speaking market. Poverty, war and persecution were the future if he stayed in Paris. He continued to write while he looked for ways to get his family out of the country. He had an idea, based on a newspaper article he had read, for a story about a forty year-old man who liked young girls and had married a woman he did not love in order to be near her twelve year-old daughter. The story would be written again in America and developed into a riveting tale: funny, touching, tragic and beautifully written, and eventually to be called *Lolita*.

By chance, a fellow writer in Paris had been offered a summer job, teaching a short course on Russian literature at Stanford University in the United States. The friend didn't want the job and recommended Vladimir for the post. Nabokov leaped at the chance to escape war-torn Europe and start his life over, yet again. But he needed papers: affidavits from prominent Russians living in America to help him obtain a visa. The émigré network swung into action and put him in touch with the right names. The French end of things was proving more difficult. The family needed exit permits to leave the country. It was Véra who trailed from office to office, trying to break through the impossible red tape of French officialdom. They had mislaid the Nabokovs' passports, she was told. Véra, resourceful as ever, played the officials' game. The moment she placed two hundred francs on a bureaucrat's desk, she was told the passports were lodged at the Ministry of the Interior. Tramping back across Paris, only to find their passports were not at the Ministry, she trudged on to the Foreign Ministry, all the time fearing she would be arrested for bribing an official. But, to her relief, the passports were there and, after two long months, Nabokov was asked to sign for them. They had their exit papers. They could go to America. But they were not there yet.

A Jewish rescue agency in the States was organising a boat to bring refugees across the Atlantic. The director of the agency was an old friend and admirer of Vladimir's father. He offered the family a cabin at half price but, still, the Nabokovs had no money for the rest of the fare. A benefit event was arranged and Vladimir gave his last public reading in Europe as a poor, relatively unknown writer. Wealthy Jewish families, as well as less well-off friends, helped raise the fare for the Nabokovs' voyage. The Germans were on their way to Paris. The Nabokovs scrambled to reach the Brittany coast, carrying a sick child with them; Dmitri was running a temperature of 104 and was in no condition to travel. Vladimir and Véra feared they would not be allowed on board if it were known that their son was ill. Dosed with a cocktail of medicines, young Dmitri was guided, a parent firmly grasping each hand, up the gang plank to freedom. The generous friends they left behind in Paris were not so lucky. Many were rounded up and died in concentration camps, including Vladimir's brother Sergei. And the ship the Nabokovs sailed on was making its last voyage. It would be sunk by German submarines on its next crossing.

Noise, heat, crowds, music. It reminded Véra of travelling across America, all those years ago. She leaned carefully over the balcony, their balcony, the one where they'd sat playing chess and watching the world go by. There was a carnival atmosphere below. The Montreux Jazz Festival was in full swing and entertainments were taking place, right there in the street. Normally, Vladimir would plan their butterfly hunting trips to coincide with this season. They were always on the move. Why, the very background of *Lolita*, with its description of pre-fabricated motel rooms and the late night cacophony of flushing toilets, came out of those long weeks on the road in America. How many thousands of miles had she driven? How many butterflies had Volodya discovered? He was a respected lepidopterist in the States, as well as an eminent professor of literature, until the storm broke over his tale of a twelve year-old girl and her stepfather. Véra smiled as she remembered. She turned to go back inside. A magnificent blue-winged *Echinargus* fluttered around her head. She started to call for Lody to come out and see, then checked herself. It's this heat, she told herself. It makes one so slow-witted. Tomorrow, she would ask Dmitri to drive her to the mountains. Now, there was a place to see butterflies.

The Nabokovs arrived in New York in style on 28 May 1940, even though they had hardly two cents to rub together. The Jewish refugee agency that had chartered their ship had allocated the family a first-class cabin in recognition of Nabokov senior's stand against anti-Semitism in Russia, all those years ago. Symbolically, the entry into their soon-to-be adopted country was a happy one, full of banter with customs officials, especially when the couple couldn't find the key to unlock one of their trunks. Even the taxi driver who took them to the apartment of Nathalie Nabokoff, Vladimir's cousin's ex-wife, was honest enough to point out their mistake when they proffered their only one hundred dollar note for the ninety cents' fare. No wonder the Nabokovs immediately filled in the paperwork that would enable them to become American citizens.

Vladimir sensed a new beginning in this land of opportunity. He finished his last novel in Russian and embraced the new culture. Whereas his friends and literary contacts in Berlin and Paris had nearly all been Russian, here Nabokov embraced the American culture and language. But he didn't forget his fellow countrymen, as they had not forgotten him in times of dire need. The composer, Rachmaninoff, had twice sent money from America to Vladimir when he was struggling in Europe. Nabokov was finding it hard to manage in the States, too, and wrote to Mikhail Chekov, nephew of the playwright, who ran a theatre company in Connecticut and would soon employ another Russian hopeful, Yul Brynner, in his group. Playwriting, or any job within reason, would do for Vladimir, as long as he could use his literary talent. After receiving a few dollars from a literary fund for Russians, Nabokov saw there was nothing for it but to return to language teaching. His New York agent made it clear that he should never write in Russian again, and he should produce thriller novels if he wanted commercial success.

But the United States would also bring other opportunities for Vladimir. Here, his passion for studying butterflies would bring him further renown in years to come. He was already corresponding with an eminent Russian lepidopterist at the Carnegie Museum in Pittsburgh and soon had his butterfly net unpacked when the family were invited to Vermont for a summer vacation. There, his cousin introduced him to the American writer and critic, Edmund Wilson, with whom Nabokov would enjoy a close literary relationship for a number of years.

The course of summer lectures at Stanford University that had allowed Vladimir and his family to escape Europe, was clearly not going to earn him much money. But he hoped the job would lead to more college teaching and he set about preparing lectures in one hundred other literary subjects: about two thousand pages of script, in all. His constant visits to museums of natural history, wherever he went, to see their butterfly collections led to research work at the American Museum of Natural History in New York. But the work was unpaid and it was Véra who landed a good secretarial job, briefly, before serious illness forced her to quit her post. Vladimir was having health problems, too, with his teeth. Finally, they were all extracted and replaced with dentures but the treatment cost money; money the Nabokovs didn't have.

The campus lecture circuit would prove to be a godsend for Vladimir. His debut as a guest lecturer in literature at Wells College, near Cornell, was a resounding success and other engagements followed, including a fortnights' lectures at Wellesley College which led to a year-long appointment. Nabokov's public readings in Europe had been a good training ground in audience communication. He was a popular speaker and regularly collected bonuses for his work. His tall, suave appearance, his old-style classic clothes, the twinkle in his eye as he spoke, had his audiences captivated. And, through Edmund Wilson, he was starting to publish short stories in *Atlantic Monthly*. His trip to Stanford on the West Coast gave him, and Véra, the opportunity to collect rare butterflies. In the Grand Canyon, Nabokov came across a species that had not been described in text books and he named it after the friend who had kindly driven them from New York to Stanford.

Only a few students enrolled for Vladimir's course but the energy he poured into his lectures set the room alight. Always a hard worker, he continued to write when he could, and sometimes read out his own fiction to students. Butterfly collecting remained a passionate hobby. Once, while chasing a specimen with his net, he trod on a sleeping bear; another time, he had to be treated for poison ivy after a day's hunting. At last, his first book in English: *The Real Life of Sebastian Knight* was accepted by a publisher, having collected rejection slips during the previous three years. The advance was small, but there was an option for three more books. He would continue to lecture at Wellesley, then Cornell University from 1948, as well as tour other campuses and do low-paid work in butterfly research for several years. His short stories would prove more popular than his novels and were published regularly in *The New Yorker*, but he was never paid much and he always had debts. There was Dmitri's education to fund, as well.

Véra worked hard for her husband. She took dictation and typed up all his work, ran a filing system and collected his press cuttings. She was his researcher, his secretary, his chauffeur, his assistant at lectures and even his replacement when he was unable to take a class himself or do butterfly research. In addition, she would take on other secretarial work. She was convinced her husband was the most talented of living writers and would eventually be recognised as such. The couple lived simply: they never bought a home or cared for possessions; their one indulgence was their son, who they adored and, eventually, they bought themselves a car. Vladimir even gave up his habit of smoking sixty cigarettes a day, which he'd enjoyed since he was a schoolboy in Russia. The cigarettes were replaced by candy and he promptly put on several stones in weight, which gave him an avuncular appearance instead of his previously lean, poetic one. But nothing affected his literary output, which was prodigious, or its refinement in content and technique, and was leading to the novel that Véra Nabokov knew her husband was born to write.

Vladimir employed index cards in his butterfly research and started to use them for writing stories, now that he was so busy teaching, enabling him to compose parts of a tale out of sequence, ready to be inserted later. But he was unhappy with the progress of his latest novel, based on the article he had read, all those years ago, about a middle-aged man who was fond of young girls. The idea was growing stale; he didn't think the story would sell very well, or even be published. He had to write for money, now. So, that was it: destroy the index cards; into the incinerator. Vladimir carried the stack of cards out to the back yard, but Véra got there first and told him to think again. Nabokov knew his wife was right. He couldn't destroy *Lolita*. He returned her to his desk and continued to work on the details of her sad tale, meticulously researching the teenage magazines she would have read, the music she would have listened to, the phrases she would have used. He added his experiences of motels across America, his impressions of members of womens' clubs where he lectured; even his trips to the dentist found their way into Humbert Humbert's confession of his misdeeds. But Nabokov continued to be short of money and needed to teach and write stories that would sell. He felt overworked, underpaid and frustrated by what little time he had to work on *Lolita*. A Guggenheim Fellowship allowed him to take some time off lecturing. The novel inched forward. He was working on the manuscript for sixteen hours a day. Finally, on 6 December 1953, the book was finished.

Hollywood screen idol, George Sanders, was not a happy man. He sulked on his West Coast boat. His marriage to the rich and famous Zsa Zsa Gabor was on the rocks and he was bored with films and the acting fraternity. He longed to devote himself to more intellectual pursuits. Books, for instance. But, since no one ever made money from writing, George knew he would have to find another, quicker path to wealth and early retirement. He went below deck and took a bottle from a locker, poured himself a drink and sat down to think.

Vladimir Nabokov realised his manuscript was dynamite. It would probably get him expelled from his university job and he might never work again. He decided the safest course of action was to submit *Lolita* under an assumed name, even though such a shocking tale might never be published. Humbert Humbert's machinations and Lolita's wiles and fancies were woven into a complex, tragic tale that would surely disturb critics and the general public alike. But Nabokov saw it as a moral story, not an obscene one. The Viking Press, to whom he had submitted the manuscript, saw it differently; *Lolita* would land them all in jail, if it were to see the light of day. Simon and Schuster thought the novel was 'sheer pornography', as did several other publishers. Vladimir put the manuscript away in a box, locked the box in his desk and concealed the desk key in another box in the middle of his filing cabinet, locked his office door and went off to New Mexico to chase butterflies.

Nabokov had felt impelled to write *Lolita* for artistic reasons. It was his twelfth novel, the culmination of decades of thought and experimentation, the best writing he had ever produced. He wanted the book to be published, whether it made money or not. In fact, he was prepared to offer an agent 25% commission to place it, even though the family finances were stretched, as usual. To help promote the book, he was advised to publish it in his own name. This seemed feasible when the manuscript began to do the rounds in France, having been rejected by a string of American publishing houses. The novel finally landed on the desk of Olympia Press in Paris, an imprint that was not afraid to publish, in English, texts that would not get past the censor in England and the States. Olympia Press was happy to take on *Lolita* but offered a low rate of royalty. Nabokov desperately wanted to see the book in print and Olympia promised to bring the novel quickly to market. He could wait no longer. On 6 June 1955, Vladimir signed on the dotted line. *Lolita* had taken two years to find a publisher and it would be another three years before the novel took off into the stratosphere.

But there were printing difficulties. Nabokov received copies of the book, late in 1955, and found it was full of typographical errors. Added to this, the copyright was in the publisher's name, as well as Nabokov's. Excerpts from the novel could not be reprinted in newspapers and periodicals because of the decency laws. It was not until the middle of January 1956 that Vladimir learned Graham Greene had listed *Lolita* in the Christmas issue of *The Sunday Times* as one of his top three books for 1955. Now the storm was about to break. At the end of January, the English columnist, John Gordon, had criticised Graham Greene in *The Sunday Express* for selecting what he called 'the filthiest book I have ever read. Sheer, unrestrained pornography ... ' Greene, ever the ironist, promptly founded, with some friends, a John Gordon Society to protect the nation's morals from 'offensive' art. Nabokov was dismayed that his book had been classed as pornography, but the matter was out of his hands. Greene's John Gordon Society met in London that March with intellectuals such as Christopher Isherwood, A. J. Ayer and Angus Wilson in attendance. The society proposed keeping Scrabble words wholesome and suggested publishers print a book band: 'Banned by the John Gordon Society', generating even more column inches on *Lolita* in Britain and abroad.

Soon, France's top publishing house, Gallimard, wanted to publish the book in French. American publishers now followed. *Lolita* began to sell like hot cakes in New York for well over its retail price. Véra used half of her husband's advance to buy herself a new gun, perhaps thinking they would need it. Nabokov had often called his feisty wife Verochka, instead of Véra, which, in

Russian, meant a boxer who went into the ring and never stopped fighting. Vervolodya was their most intimate name for themselves as a couple. People who met them marvelled at the Nabokovs' closeness, their almost telepathic communication, their *tendresse*. They were likened to butterflies mating behind a bush, quickly parting before anyone had realised they were making love.

While Vladimir worried about losing his job, the press fanned the flames of the *Lolita* scandal and publishers scrambled for translation rights. The book was banned in the courts of England and France, then the ban was lifted. Nabokov was now a world-famous writer and, instead of being fired from his job, he received offers for other prestigious academic posts. His university salary soared. His lectures attracted huge crowds. At one venue, the lecture hall was so packed that Vladimir and Véra couldn't find a parking place. Finally, they found one some distance away and raced to the hall, with members of their audience scooting past them, unaware they were overtaking the speaker.

At last, after copyright discussions with Olympia Press, *Lolita* was published in the United States to sensational reviews. Stanley Kubrick wanted the film rights. Vladimir now had a Hollywood agent. Véra's faith in her husband's writing was finally vindicated. Although she believed his talent should have been recognised decades earlier, they both agreed the money he was now earning, after years of penny-pinching, was welcome. In January 1959, the Nabokovs took a sabbatical that would turn into academic retirement. From now on, Vladimir would focus on writing full-time, as well as his beloved butterflies. He yearned to see Europe again. His sister,

Elena, was now living in Geneva. And there was a small matter of taxation to attend to. Vladimir had landed himself in the seventy per cent tax bracket and his lawyers recommended a trust fund. The Nabokovs packed their bags and caught a boat back to France. No longer the poverty-stricken refugees who'd arrived from war-torn Europe, they were rich, famous, intellectually admired and feted, and thinking of retirement. George Sanders was on his way to Geneva, too, and planning his own version of early retirement.

The balcony door was becoming difficult for Véra to open now. The evening air seemed to chill. She wouldn't linger, she told herself. Just say a few words. She liked talking to herself, these days. At least, *they* thought that was what she was doing, those who watched over her. It was her secret; she was communing with Volodya. He'd always felt life did not end with death. They'd discussed it. Life went on, in some shape or form. And there was the light blue butterfly flitting above her again. Her eyes were poor now, but she was sure she had seen it, or one just like it, on the balcony before.

    She spoke to it: 'Volodya – Volodya, they say I have to move from here. I have a feeling I'll never come back. I'm tired, my darling. I miss you. We did everything together, didn't we? Tell me, can I fly away with you now, across the lake to the mountains?' She turned her head to listen. She'd had such trouble with her hearing lately. Was that the traffic below? Car brakes, horns? She thought she heard someone call 'Verochka!'

The Nabokovs arrived in France in October 1959, and went straight on to Geneva to visit Vladimir's sister. They saw *Lolita* displayed in every book shop window in at least three languages. After ten days, they took the train to Paris and were given all the media attention that Georges Simenon had received on his return to Europe, four years earlier. The publisher Gallimard gave Vladimir a reception of two thousand people: the world's literary VIPs were there. Nabokov was more at ease in France's Musée d'Histoire Naturelle, looking at butterfly specimens. Then it was on to London where they had dinner with Graham Greene, first public champion of *Lolita*, and who Vladimir found very entertaining. He lectured at his old university at Cambridge with great success, then set off for Rome. But the paparazzi followed the Nabokovs through the streets and they fled to Sicily in search of peace and quiet. Vladimir wanted to write. But the press hounded them there, too, and the couple moved on to Genoa where the author found peace, at last.

But Nabokov found Europe had changed and the couple returned to the States. They travelled to California, where Vladimir worked on his screenplay of *Lolita* for Stanley Kubrick. Like George Sanders, the Nabokovs were at not at ease with the Hollywood party scene, but they were happy with Kubrick's choice of Sue Lyon for the role of Lolita and Shelley Winters as the unfortunate Charlotte Haze. Once again, Vladimir saw his lawyers about his tax situation. In November 1960, he and Véra boarded the *Queen Elizabeth* for Europe. They headed for the South of France, searching for somewhere quiet where Vladimir could write. Though the Nabokovs would always consider themselves American citizens, their stock market returns had been poor and they thought about buying land in Switzerland. Stanley Kubrick had advised Peter Ustinov to settle there after they'd worked together on *Spartacus* and the director thought Nabokov well-advised to follow his fellow Russian into tax exile.

The couple holidayed in Champex in Valais, while Vladimir wrote and hunted butterflies, before driving on to Montreux. They had a vague notion they would rent or buy a home there, or in Geneva or Lausanne. In Switzerland Nabokov could continue his interest in alpine butterflies, and they would be close to their son, Dmitri, who was now an opera singer in Milan. Peter Ustinov recommended the Montreux Palace Hotel to Vladimir and Véra. The film star was living there, himself, with his family while they looked around for a more permanent home. It was settled: the Nabokovs moved into the rooms below the Ustinovs in August 1961. But, unlike Peter and his family, the Nabokovs would not be moving on.

Montreux was the ideal base for Vladimir: the town was fairly quiet but cosmopolitan, with international newspapers on sale every day, and he was not far from the mountains where he could chase butterflies. Montreux's micro-climate, with the sun reflecting off the lake and the mountains shielding the town from the chilly alpine winds, seemed perfect for the Nabokovs. Vladimir wasn't sure he wanted to hear Peter Ustinov's feet crossing the floor in the suite above them, but the Ustinovs built a house in Les Diablerets and the Nabokovs moved upstairs into the vacated apartment. Vladimir would often sit in the gardens by the lake and write on his index cards. The hotel was perfect for the couple's needs: they had no home to maintain, no possessions to worry about. Véra would deal with her husband's correspondence and his contracts, leaving him time to read and write. Since *Lolita*, the author had become big business. He would sign himself 'VN' and Véra would refer to him as such when talking business on the phone. She would field his calls and vet his visitors, take dictation and do research. In the evenings, after dinner, the couple would sit on the balcony of their suite, playing chess and watching the sunset on the Dents du Midi across the lake. They would retire early but Vladimir, ever the insomniac, would often wake and write in the night.

Peter Ustinov was filming in the adjoining studio at Elstree in England when Kubrick was filming *Lolita*. The actor looked in on the set and was happy to report to Vladimir that the production was going well. The Nabokovs returned to New York for the film première in 1962 and had dinner with their future neighbour, James Mason. But they were soon back in Switzerland where life had become so comfortable. They bought a small parcel of land next to Peter Ustinov's much larger plot, but they never built the small chalet they had planned to put there. They would simply book themselves into mountain hotels or rent an apartment for the summer so that Vladimir could chase butterflies.

But he was not as agile as he had been in his youth. He was seventy-six, had weight problems and was taking strong medication for his insomnia. His youngest brother had died of a heart attack in 1964 and Nabokov, himself, was advised by his doctors to continue walking along the lake for exercise in the winter. Both he and Véra had several bouts of ill-health and, once, while chasing butterflies in the mountains at Davos, Vladimir fell down a steep slope, losing hold of his butterfly net which wedged in a fir tree below. Reaching out to retrieve the net, he fell even further and, this time, was unable to get up. At last, a cable car rumbled overhead. Passengers looked down at the old man in shorts on the ground below, smiling and waving at them. On the cable car's return journey, the operator noticed the man was still lying there and raised the alarm at the end of his run. Two and a half hours after his fall, Vladimir was stretchered off the mountain. No bones were broken and, after several days in bed and some weeks of recuperation, he was out, chasing butterflies once more. But he seemed less robust than before his accident and, when he returned from his holiday to Montreux, he knew he was unwell.

At Montreux Hospital, tests showed he had a tumour on the prostate. The next day, he was operated on at the Clinique de Montchoisi and the tumour was found to be benign. But, against his doctor's advice, he continued working on his new novel, which slowed his recovery. A mild, post-op infection didn't help, or the ineffectiveness of his sleeping pills after years of taking so many each night. A week after his seventy-seventh birthday, in April 1976, Nabokov fell in his bathroom and was rushed, concussed, to the cantonal hospital at Lausanne. Ten days later, he returned to Montreux but found it difficult to walk. His temperature rose and he developed an infection and fell into a state of semi-consciousness.

Back in the Clinique de Montchoisi, Nabokov suffered bouts of delirium and was moved back to the cantonal hospital where Véra and Dmitri hired private nurses to watch over him around the clock. Véra's concern for her husband was not helped by the extreme pain she was in, having damaged her spine trying to prevent his fall in the bathroom. When he was released from hospital, they convalesced together at the luxurious Valmont Clinic at Glion, in the mountains above Montreux, but Vladimir found walking a difficult business now; he was weak from his hospitalisations and too exhausted to work. With an effort, he rallied the following spring and, using a cane, he managed a few yards' walking with his son along the Grand Rue.

But his constitution remained weak and he caught a bad dose of influenza from Dmitri. The 'flu developed into bronchial pneumonia and, again, Nabokov was hospitalised, this time for seven weeks. When he returned to Montreux in May 1977, he appeared to his friends a hunched and wizened old man. Yet, he seemed in good spirits until June, when his delirium returned and his temperature rose again. He was rushed back to Lausanne and hospitalised. Despite antibiotics and rest, he grew weaker. Véra and Dmitri were constantly at his bedside, fearing the worst. But Vladimir seemed resigned to his decline, no longer able to fight it. When Dmitri kissed his father goodnight on the forehead, as he had always done, two days before the end, Nabokov looked tearful and unhappy. His son asked him what was wrong. A particular butterfly was now on the wing, explained his father. He knew he would never see it again. His temperature rose and his bronchial infection worsened. At 6.50 p.m. on the evening of 2 July 1977, Vladimir Nabokov moaned three times, then ceased to breathe.

Nabokov was cremated a few days later in Vevey and his ashes were buried in Clarens cemetery, in the shadow of Château du Châtelard, close to his great aunt Praskovia-Alexandria Nabokov (1837-1909), née Tolstoy. Charlie Chaplin's brother, Sydney, and his wife, Gypsy, are buried nearby, too. Véra stayed on at the Montreux Palace Hotel, devoting herself to her husband's work until her own health began to fail. In 1990, extensive renovations to the Edwardian hotel obliged Véra to move to an apartment on the hill, closer to her husband's grave, yet in sight of the hotel where she and Vladimir had enjoyed the rewards of years of hardship and hard work.

The screen idol, George Sanders, whose life had begun in Russia in similar circumstances to Nabokov's, never regained the wealth and lifestyle the two men had been born to inherit. The actor suffered a series of strokes, took an overdose in 1972 and, like Nabokov, never saw Russia again. Véra Nabokov died on 6 April 1991 at Vevey, in the same hospital as Graham Greene, the writer who had championed her husband's work and who had died there three days earlier. Véra's ashes were buried with Vladimir's in the cemetery by the sloping vineyards at Clarens, not far from their beloved hotel balcony and the mountains beyond.

The door to the balcony swung open and a blonde, fashionably-dressed woman stepped gaily into the sunshine. She spread her manicured nails over the top of the gilt railing and leaned forward to take in the holiday crowds below. She wanted to laugh out loud at the huge bronze statue of Vladimir Nabokov, sitting in his butterfly-hunting knickerbockers in the gardens below, but that last lift had left her facial muscles a little restricted. She shifted her gaze, taking in the thick tops of the trees, the exotic flowers, the sun's reflection on the water. 'Gee, Harry, look at this!' she suddenly cried.

A gruff voice answered her from inside the hotel suite. 'For God's sake, Barbara – I don't want to see another goddam mountain this trip. OK?'

'No, come look, Harry! There's two gorgeous butterflies out here, just sunning themselves on the rail.'

There was a moment's silence, then something like an impatient sigh. 'You wanna do your shopping now, before lunch?'

'Their wings! What a beautiful colour! I'd love a dress that shade of blue – '

'You comin', Barb? I need a beer. A cold one.'

'Oh, Harry, they've taken off! They're dancing round each other, just like lovers on the wing ... '

'I'm telling you, Barbara, it's a quarter past already. You wanna look at watches, or what?'

Chapter 6
Freddie Mercury

A cloudless night. The moon, full and bright at three in the morning, drenches the french windows in a silver light, illuminating an old man behind the glass, hunched over his lectern, working carefully in pencil on a Russian text. He stops writing for a moment and lifts his head, searching for *le mot juste*, *la phrase*, to describe the unspoken tension between two of his characters. Ah, yes! Ivan rose and regarded Katrina with eyes like glowing coals –

'WHEEOAUGH!'

Nabokov stiffened, blinked and put down his pencil. Suddenly, the floor beneath him began to shudder. Was it the water pipes? The hotel heating system? Or were the Alps on the move? Vladimir shuffled in his carpet slippers over to the door of his wife's bedroom. He tapped urgently on the top panel. The door opened immediately.

'Véra!' the writer spoke in a hushed voice, although he was sure the whole of the Montreux Palace Hotel must have been wakened by the noise he'd just heard. 'What on earth is happening? There's the most dreadful sound coming from the suite below – '

'WHEY-HEYEE!'

Edwardian floorboards groaned beneath the Nabokovs. The couple stood, looking at each other for a moment. Then Véra's sleepy eyes lit up and she smiled at her husband. 'You know, there's a pop star in town. I saw him in the lift tonight. A nice young man, very polite – '

'A pop star! In this hotel!' spluttered Vladimir. 'What is the world coming to? Well, he can't afford to stay here for long, that's for sure!'

'He probably has more money than we have ... '

'Hmm,' her husband shook his head in disbelief and returned to his lectern. 'That depends where he pays his taxes ...' he muttered, taking up his pencil again.

A graunching sound issued from below. 'WHAAAGH!'

The pencil was replaced on the lectern. 'How can I compose with that racket going on? You know how easily my concentration is disturbed. I remember Peter Ustinov's footsteps – Now, listen to that! It sounds as though someone is swinging from the chandelier!'

'I think that might be the case,' his wife wrapped her dressing gown around her and tied the belt in a loose knot. 'Would you like some tea, Volodya dear?'

The colourful, exotic, outrageous life of Farrokh Bulsara, known to millions of rock fans as Freddie Mercury, began on 5 September 1946 on the spice island of Zanzibar, off the East African coast of Tanzania. Like the Nabokov family in pre-revolutionary Russia, the Bulsaras were part of a ruling class that enjoyed a privileged existence before violent revolution overturned their lives. Fortunately for Freddie, by the time this bloody event took place, he had acquired, like Vladimir Nabokov, a self-confidence which would propel him forward, despite setbacks that would have stifled ambition in most people.

The Bulsara family were Indian Parsees of Persian origin, one of a number of British Indian families who settled on Zanzibar during the island's half century as a British Protectorate. Bomi Bulsara, Freddie's father, was a civil servant, a British Government High Court cashier who brought his wife, Jer, to the island to enjoy a comfortable life in the coastal capital of Stone Town. Brought up with a nanny and servants, Freddie would be at ease with an entourage of staff and helpers in later years. Like Nabokov, he was the all-important first son, born into a certain social class. And, like the Russian writer, his formative years would be spent in a world that would soon cease to exist. But change was what Freddie Mercury was all about.

He was a bundle of contradictions from the start: polite and mischievous in turns, a shy little boy who shone in class. He could read and write and do arithmetic with ease, but drawing, painting and modelwork were his all-absorbing interests. At the age of eight, along with many boys from his background, Freddie was sent to India, to a boarding school based on the British system. The experience would make him a British patriot for life and a fan of the royal family. The name he gave his rock band, Queen, would say it all, and a lot more besides.

St Peter's Church of England boarding school in Panchgani, not far from Bombay, was young Bulsara's first test in self-sufficiency, although he had relatives living close by who would look after him in the school holidays. Like most new boarders, Freddie cried himself softly to sleep in the dormitory, at first, pining for his mother and younger sister. But he knew he could not show any weakness that might alert the school bullies. He joined the existing system, for the one and only time in his life, and made the best of it. Soon, school friends and teachers alike began to call him Freddie, an anglicised version of Farrokh, then his family took up the name, too. Yet, although he had friends, Freddie was never one of the crowd, in class or on the sports field. He was an individualist and would excel most of all at solo activities, such as art and music. But he loved cricket and received the school Junior All-Rounder Trophy, and was also, like Vladimir Nabokov, a good boxer, nimble on his feet. At ten, he was the school table tennis champion and an excellent sprinter and hockey player. But painting and drawing remained Freddie's first loves, keeping him apart from his classmates in his spare time.

It was Freddie's head teacher, Mr Davis, who first noticed the boy's love of music, both classical and contemporary, and wrote to Mr and Mrs Bulsara, suggesting extra music tuition for their son. Freddie was already listening to the western pop music of the 1950s, as well as Indian music and classical works. He particularly liked opera and he loved singing. He adored his piano lessons and practised in the holidays, passing exams in theory and practice up to Grade IV, encouraged by an old Irish lady with wild hair called Miss O'Shea. He also sang in the school choir, which the day girls were allowed to join. Freddie was fond of girls, particularly a classmate called Gita. Until then, his world of close relationships, outside of his family, had been male-orientated.

Freddie was known to his friends as Bucky. There were simply too many teeth in his mouth and the front ones stuck out, making him so self-conscious that he would put his hand up to his face whenever he laughed. But this did not stop him strutting the boards regularly in school plays and, because he was such a good actor, he could manage female roles much better than other boys and often took the part of a girl in a production. His ability on stage and his creative ideas in art and music led him to form a pop group with his classmates, called The Hectics. He had often sung on the school stage before, and had won the Junior section of a school singing competition. Now, he and his like-minded set of friends practised assiduously, first in their dormitory, then in the school music room. Soon, with Freddie pounding the ivories, the group were playing at school fetes, concerts and other occasions with admiring females screaming at the band in true pop fashion. But it was the lead guitarist who took centre stage on these occasions. Shy young Bucky stayed out of the spotlight, honing his skills to be the next Fats Domino or Little Richard.

After a while, Freddie began to lose interest in his academic work and immerse himself in his art and music. He grew thin and intense and called people 'Darling'. He was becoming the perfect aesthete. His parents brought him home to Zanzibar in 1962 where he spent two years at a Catholic convent school, completing his education. But it was clear that the British would soon withdraw from the island. Revolution was in the air. It had begun with Britain's loss of her colonies after the Second World War. First India and Pakistan gained their independence, then Burma and Ceylon followed. The Communist upheavals in China strongly influenced a national movement in East Africa and anti-British sentiment soon spread to Zanzibar. Workers and unions turned themselves into political parties and in 1956, the Zanzibar National Party was formed. By 1963, strikes and riots led to the British bowing out of the region, and a political coup by Africans soon followed. In the carnage, thousands of Indians and Arabs were murdered and many more were forced to leave the island. In 1964, Bomi Bulsara and his family fled Zanzibar with only a few suitcases. They headed for England where relatives took them in. Freddie was seventeen years of age. Vladimir Nabokov had been nineteen when he had sailed away from Russia, under fire. Like Nabokov, Freddie would never see his homeland again. Unlike Nabokov, he would never talk about the experience.

Feltham, in the West London borough of Hounslow, close to Heathrow Airport, was where the Bulsaras made their home in England. They found a Victorian terraced house close to the relatives with whom they had first stayed and

Bomi went to work as an accountant for the catering firm Forte. Freddie knew his future had to be a creative one, and in September 1964 he enrolled at the local polytechnic to get the necessary qualification he would need for art school. He easily gained an A grade in A level Art and went on to study for a Diploma in Graphic Art and Design at Ealing College of Art in the autumn of 1966. These were the heady years of the Swinging Sixties in London. Freddie could not have been better placed to embark on a bohemian lifestyle. His level of education, charm and wit, his slim, effete appearance and flamboyant style of dress all combined to give him an Oscar Wilde - Aubrey Beardsley type of appearance. He blossomed in the artistic environment of college, wearing the latest tight, colourful clothes in fashionable crushed velvets and suedes, and listening to the new and experimental music coming out of London and the west coast of America.

It was natural that Freddie would want to leave home and put suburbia and its values behind him. It didn't matter that he would have to commute back to Ealing to finish his Diploma course; he needed to live in a part of London where fashion and music and the hippest people were all around him, bringing him cultural stimulation. He rented a small flat in Kensington, home of the famous Biba emporium and close to Carnaby Street in Soho and Chelsea's King's Road. Life took off for Freddie after college hours, making him slightly bored with his studies and more inclined to 'hang out' in the college restaurant in his snakeskin shoes and gorgeous scarves and consciously-styled clothes. He adored the American musician Jimi Hendrix, his original music and dandified appearance, and would spend hours sketching portraits of his hero. Artistic originality would always impress Freddie and he would strive for the same in his own innovative career.

With a like-minded college friend, Freddie would while away his study hours singing harmonies for fun, using his ruler as a microphone. He would drop into parties where friends were playing the blues and listen to their music. An idea was forming in his head, though he continued his studies. Freddie had almost decided to make music his career. He attended a friend's pop group rehearsal at Imperial College, resulting in an instant rapport with the lead guitarist, physics and astronomy student Brian May, and Roger Taylor, drummer and dentistry student and third future member of Queen. The young musicians had called their band Smile, which seemed to be a happy omen. On stage, they supported the big names of Sixties rock: Pink Floyd, T. Rex and Yes. They enjoyed Freddie's company, his enthusiasm and his humour, and it wasn't long before he was turning up at their performances and giving them advice on how they should present themselves. Freddie knew instinctively that presentation counted, that it sold a product. Soon, Roger gave up his dentistry degree and went into business with Freddie, selling way-out clothes at exorbitant prices in Kensington market. These were happy days for Freddie, he was in his element: the chat, the charm, the clothes, the crowd, the camaraderie of the group and his ideas for the future. He was well-known in the market place, dashing about the stalls in his foppish dress and with his loud voice, calling people 'dalling'. All Freddie needed now was the opportunity to be famous, and he was convinced that would happen soon.

But Smile faded, in spite of a recording contract and Freddie's best efforts, for he was travelling with the group now. The group disbanded. Brian, Roger, and several other musicians and girlfriends were living a hand-to-mouth existence in a squalid flat in Barnes when Freddie moved in with them. There were many discussions about their future, with Freddie telling his flatmates what he would do to improve their chances of success if he were their lead singer. He was already singing with a Liverpudlian group called Ibex but his flamboyant stage persona was making this conservative band uneasy. One night, as he swung his microphone too energetically in the air, he lost the bottom half of it. From then on, the baton-style mike became part of his act. He was already strutting his stuff for the audience like a superstar, but Ibex was going nowhere. Freddie rechristened the group Wreckage. And soon, they were all washed up.

The singer was now looking for another group to front, and guitarist Brian and drummer Roger were looking for a good vocalist. Freddie's voice was strong, harmonious and operatic and his stage act was already memorable. Stick thin, he could manoeuvre himself into the skimpiest hand-made trousers, barely able to sit down in them while waiting to go onstage but, once on the boards, he was lithe and prancing. In April 1970, the three flatmates came up with a name for their new group. It was Freddie's choice, insisting that a one-word name was stronger than two or three words, which would dilute any impact. Brian and Roger weren't so sure. The word 'queen' had homosexual connotations. Freddie saw that as an advantage. The name was double-edged: regal, yet camp.

It wasn't long before Roger and Brian, with their strongly heterosexual reputations, could see the amusing side of this. And so could Freddie; he could twirl and pose on the stage to his heart's content. He was balletic, his feet were winged. He was Mercury, the winged messenger of the Gods. From now on, he would be known as the charismatic Freddie Mercury.

If Freddie was confused about his sexuality, he had no doubts about his feelings for a petite blonde called Mary Austin whom Brian introduced him to, that same year. Freddie fell in love with this elfin girl and they set up home together. Mary worked at Biba's, one of London's top boutiques in the Swinging Sixties. She knew about fashion and she had a head for business. Freddie would always love and trust her. And Mary Austin would always love Freddie, though her feelings for him would be sorely tested. Mary would eventually want children, but Freddie preferred cats and the couple kept several of them in their Kensington flat. It was a breathtakingly creative period for Freddie. He was focussed and hardworking. On one occasion, he woke up in the night with an idea for a song, dragged his piano to the bedside and composed the tune while Mary – well, she became used to that sort of behaviour. It was Freddie's increasingly homosexual relationships in the late seventies that would finally split the couple. But Mary would always be there for Freddie as his personal assistant, managing his affairs and getting on with her own life. And Freddie would always call Mary his common-in-law wife. When he died, he left virtually everything to Mary.

Freddie had a theory that the harder you worked, the luckier you were. Success, he realised, was not a matter of chance but thousands of hours of concentrated effort, honing skills, polishing talent, being ready when an opportunity presented itself. He also knew the value of originality, of composing one's own material, as well as learning the practical side of the business by going on the road. He saw two sides to the music industry: the creative side that took place in a recording studio and, what he called, 'the hard sell': the months of touring and performing after an album had been made. Touring was where the band learned to play together and there was no substitute for that experience. The tension in their dressing room before a live performance would be palpable, the fallout after a show could be vociferous if someone had made an error onstage. There were dramatic arguments at a creative level; it was how the group sparked off each other. Rows could escalate and there would sometimes be talk of disbanding. But, deep down, the four musicians knew their strength lay in the group, rather than their individual talents.

Queen was not the overnight success that some people imagine. Their first three years together were a series of hopes dashed, encounters with business sharks and a continual lack of the recognition they craved. But they persevered. They now had an excellent bass guitarist, John Deacon, another university student, this time in electronics, and a wizard with the group's electrical equipment. But the record deals weren't coming their way, at least not at the level Queen felt was due to a band on its way to the top. At last, they signed a contract which they thought was right for them, without reading the small print. It would take years of wrangling and a lot of money to extricate the group from that agreement.

All four musicians were perfectionists and their compositions took a long time to produce, with the numerous over-dubs, re-mixes and finer adjustments that the group insisted on. Their first long-playing record, suitably entitled *Queen*, was released in 1973. The band toured as the warm-up act for Mott the Hoople later that year, and were a hit with the audiences. But their album was not a resounding success, and it was back to the studio where *Queen II* was produced in 1974. Sales were better this time, with Freddie's composition *Seven Seas of Rhye* making the Top Ten but, still, the big time eluded the group. It was not until their third LP, *Sheer Heart Attack*, was released with Freddie's music hall song about a high-class prostitute: *Killer Queen* making all the charts and turning gold in America, that Queen saw they were, at last, on their way to stardom.

Freddie took a lot of time and trouble over his glitzy stage appearance. His hair was styled by his personal hairdresser, his nail varnish was black, his stage outfits were shimmering leotards and, soon, he had his own masseur, in keeping with his star status. The press was suspicious of such a beautiful creature, but the crowds loved him. Freddie stopped giving interviews to the hostile British media and concentrated on pleasing the fans, and they repaid him in spades. The money was starting to come in. Finally, Freddie felt secure enough to give up his market stall in Kensington and the rest of the group gave up their studies and the grants they'd survived on.

Queen hit the road, clothed in designer Zandra Rhodes's finest. Japan went wild for them, South America had never seen anything like it and their reception was, literally, presidential. America loved them. Bodyguards were issued to each member of the group to keep thousands of adoring fans at bay. The band produced one original song after another, drawing on gospel, opera, boogie and other music genres, each composition destined to be a classic. Queen's fourth album, *A Night at the Opera*, came out in November 1975 and included John Deacon's *You're My Best Friend* and Freddie's multi-harmonied *Bohemian Rhapsody*: a heady concoction of rock, opera, baroque and ballad as complex in content as the composer himself. *Bohemian Rhapsody* won both an Ivor Novello Award and the Britannia Award for Freddie while the group was already working on their *A Day at the Races* LP with its gospel choir-style rendering of Freddie's *Somebody To Love*; he had always admired the music of Aretha Franklin. Their 1977 album, *News of the World*, included the winner's song *We Are The Champions*, written by Freddie with football fans in mind. His composition *Crazy Little Thing Called Love* was composed, unusually for Mercury, on the guitar; he was usually happier at the piano. The track was included on Queen's 1980 album *The Game*, which also featured their disco hit *Another One Bites The Dust. Flash Gordon*, Roger Taylor's *Radio Ga-Ga*, Freddie's *I Was Born To Love You* and many other hits would follow down the years. But life or, rather, the group's financial affairs were spinning out of control. Queen needed a man in a suit, someone they could trust.

Enter lawyer Jim Beach, who would extricate the musicians from various agreements and enable them to manage their business in their own way. Jim was a legal eagle in the music trade and, from 1977, he handled Queen's affairs, including Freddie's personal business to the end, and beyond. With British super-tax at 83% of income, tax avoidance was now a major consideration. In 1978, the group worked in several countries on their new album *Jazz*. When the band arrived at Mountain Studios in the lakeside resort of Montreux in Switzerland, Freddie immediately fell in love with the scenic town and its breathtaking views across the water to the Alps. The group were delighted with the sound quality of the studio and named their album after the annual Montreux Jazz Festival which was in full swing at the time. But the town seemed relatively quiet, compared to the bustle and night life of their usual haunts, and, at first, the band found it difficult to be creative in the casino complex by the lake. But Freddie enjoyed walking the ten minutes from his hotel to the studios without being mobbed. In Montreux, Queen were seen as businessmen, going about their work. Queen bought Mountain Studios in 1978, as a sound investment in every sense. David Bowie lived nearby and would join Freddie on the *Hot Space* album and many other artists, such as Status Quo, Yes, Iggy Pop and The Rolling Stones would use the studios.

Although there were moments when the group thought of going their separate ways, they worked on solo projects as a way of renewing their creativity. The talented Freddie even thought of becoming a part-time actor when he saw his friend David Bowie treading the boards in New York. Instead, he embarked on a project with the Royal

Ballet Company for a gala night on behalf of the City of Westminster Society for Mentally Handicapped Children. Freddie practised furiously at the barre with the company, pushing himself until every muscle in his body ached. But the night was a resounding success and Freddie received a standing ovation for his dancing and leaping into the air while singing in his powerful voice as the dancers caught him in their arms. Opera was another of Freddie's passions, and the night he heard the Spanish soprano, Montserrat Caballé, sing at Covent Garden Opera House, he was completely in awe of her. He was amazed, then nervous, when she agreed to sing with him and record an album, as well. When the record was released, ten thousand singles of their duet 'Barcelona' were sold in Spain in under three hours, and the couple went on to perform onstage together, including for the King and Queen of Spain. But it was Freddie's contribution to Bob Geldof's global event, Live Aid, for the starving millions in Ethiopia, that captured the hearts of so many and for which he will always be remembered.

It was one of Freddie's most memorable performances. He had the world in the palms of his hands, clapping with him to *Radio Ga-Ga*. The date was 13 July 1985 and the venue was Wembley Stadium in London. The world's top musicians had gathered for an event that would be televised live to billions of people around the world. The opening act was to be Queen: less than twenty minutes in front of a Saturday afternoon crowd, no special effects or lighting, no sound check – just get out there, play and sing, get off, next act on. But Queen, ever the professionals, understood their act would be showcased around the world. Not for them a slow amble onstage, a few strummed guitar chords and some mumbled lyrics. They spent the previous week at the Shaw Theatre on the Euston Road, honing their act to perfection. When Freddie Mercury took the stage to kick off the Live Aid concert, his rapport with the audience of hundreds of thousands was instant. He carried them with him through a medley of Queen songs, lifting their spirits and voices as they sang and clapped along with him. Everyone, musicians and commentators alike, agreed it was Freddie's finest moment. Sales of Queen's records surged around the world, and so did that of pop music in general. Freddie's performance became the stuff of legend. Francis Rossi of Status Quo, another top group who had performed that day, remembers Queen being the best act of the whole event.

Status Quo and Queen were old friends; they had spent time together in Montreux, recording at Mountain Studios and going out on the town in the evenings. Though the night life in Switzerland was relatively low-key, Queen took Status Quo to their favourite Mexican restaurant, just off the Grand Rue, where the evening kicked off with pitchers of Tequila Marguerita and continued after that. It was during Freddie's wild period, at the height of Queen's success, that he felt inspired to swing from a chandelier in the Montreux Palace Hotel. Many pop groups held after-gig parties in their hotel suites; they could afford to pay for any damage incurred by their high jinks but, naturally, they were not popular with other hotel guests. Queen were famous for their parties, during and after concerts. The British press, in particular, had a field day with lurid tales of Queen's all-night raves where most tastes in entertainment were catered for. Freddie and Mary Austin were no longer sharing a flat and Freddie had embarked on a series of gay affairs, some of which were emotionally turbulent to the point of violence. One lover in New York had to be escorted from Freddie's apartment building by security men; another, a restaurateur Freddie had met during his wild days and nights in Munich, had lost his mind and died of AIDS, a disease that could be sexually transmitted and was taking the lives of many homosexual men in the nineteen-eighties.

The London DJ and music critic, Paul Gambaccini, bumped into his friend, Freddie, at a club one evening and asked him how he was managing his social life, now that the gay scene was changing. The ebullient Mercury declared he would rather live for the moment and enjoy himself to the full, than change his attitude to sex. Gambaccini had a sad feeling that Freddie would soon be another of his friends to succumb to the AIDS disease. But Freddie had an insatiable appetite for every experience. He had success and money and could buy anything he desired. Mary found him a beautiful home in Kensington: Garden Lodge, on which he lavished thousands of pounds in restoration and redecoration costs. He installed his friends Peter Freestone, his valet and personal organiser, as well as his ex-lover, Joe Fanelli, to cook for him, plus a number of much-loved cats. Mary had an office in the house so that she could take care of Freddie's paperwork while she led her own life a few streets away. In the mid-eighties, Freddie met his last lover, Jim Hutton, a barber at the Savoy hotel. The Irishman moved into Garden Lodge and lived with the singer for the last six years of his life.

True to his word, Freddie enjoyed life to the full. He spent his money freely, on himself and others. In fact, buying presents for his friends gave him more pleasure than anything else. He would sweep into Cartier's or Tiffany's and buy gifts for no reason at all. He loved to see the look on people's faces as they unwrapped their presents. He also followed auction sales and devoured the catalogues of the big auction houses. He would acquire many beautiful things, such as paintings and ceramics and Japanese netsuke, and display them in his home. He kept an excellent wine cellar and imported his favourite dry white wine by the case from St Saphorin in Switzerland. When recording in Montreux, Freddie would rent a beautiful house on Lake Geneva called Les Cygnes, where he could gaze at the baby swans on the lake. Freddie rechristened the place Duck House, which prompted drummer Roger to call it Duckingham Palace. All of the group loved to play around with words. The recording tapes for *Radio Ga-Ga* were labelled and put on a shelf as Radio Ca-Ca. Everyone in Freddie's inner circle was given a gender name-change. Peter was known as Phoebe, Joe Fanelli as Liza, after Ms Minelli, Mary as Steve, after the Six Million Dollar Man, Steve Austin, Brian May naturally became Maggie and Roger Taylor, Liz. Freddie went by the name of Melina, after the Greek actress, Ms Mercouri. Even the outer circle could not escape being nicknamed: Cliff Richard, whose records had earned him so many silver discs, was called Sylvia Disc and Neil Sedaka, whose records invariably went gold, was Golda Disc.

As the years went by and the group mellowed and found long-term partners, Scrabble became the after-gig pastime of choice. Games were serious and lasted all night in hotel rooms. In the recording studio, teams of players, comprising of everyone from the tea-maker to mega-stars, participated in the game during the long hours of album-making. Freddie was a serious player and adept at placing words in the most effective place. Innuendo was a favourite word of his, and it became the title of the penultimate album he recorded in Montreux. The group's legal manager, Jim Beach, already lived in Montreux and was able to introduce Freddie to the good life in the area. Freddie was impressed with Frédy Giradet's world-famous restaurant in the old village of Crissier, near Lausanne, though he was not a big eater at the best of times. As he gradually became unwell, he would eat even less and his household staff found it difficult to tempt him to eat anything at all. It was apparent to everyone that he was seriously ill, but Freddie would not discuss his health with anyone.

He had suffered from throat nodules since over-straining his voice in the early days of his career. Surgeons had wanted to operate, but Freddie was nervous about the outcome. He had always been a fit person, but now he was resting more and touring less, partying less, avoiding red wine and sticking to champagne. Queen's open-air performance at Knebworth Park on 9 August 1986 was to be their last gig, although no one realised it at the time. The stars were out that night, including The Rolling Stones and Led Zeppelin, but Freddie melted away after the show, missing the usual party and heading back to London with his partner, Jim Hutton.

Freddie officially tested positive for AIDS in 1987, but he'd had his suspicions long before that. Many of his friends and lovers had died. He had lost one hundred acquaintances in Munich alone; ex-lovers in New York were no longer alive. Joe Fanelli, his cook and ex-lover was ill, so was the band's ex-personal manager, Paul Prenter. Prenter would eventually go to the British press and receive a great deal of money for the tales he told about Freddie. The press now maintained a presence outside his London home. Montreux became a haven where the singer could find peace, away from the limelight, and continue to collaborate with the band. The other musicians could see he was ill but no one wanted to broach the subject. They waited for Freddie to explain the situation in his own way, which he finally did. He had less energy now, but he channelled his creativity into his singing and continued to make videos, using makeup to disguise his gaunt appearance.

During those last years, Freddie spent a lot of time recording in Montreux and, in spite of the fact that he knew time was limited, he decided to make a home for himself there. He would have liked to have bought Duck House, but the owner did not want to sell at that time. Instead, Jim Beach found him a penthouse apartment in the beautiful *belle époque* building, Les Tourelles, on the waterfront. The balconied residence on the Quai des Fleurs, with its marble-walled foyer and stunning views across the lake to the Alps was to be Freddie's last interior decoration project. It was also the subject of his last birthday cake, skilfully made by the actress and cake-maker Jane Asher from photographs of the apartment taken by Jim Beach and Joe Fanelli.

There was a delay over the transference of the lease for the flat, but that did not stop Freddie launching himself into yet another buying spree in order to furnish the place. Beds and linen were bought in Montreux and auction catalogues were studied assiduously. Antique furniture and paintings were purchased from Sotheby's and Christie's. An Empire suite for the salon went straight from the auction room to the re-upholsterer's and then to Montreux. But, coming out of Bonhams auction room in South Kensington, Freddie missed his footing on the marble steps and was only prevented from falling headlong by his valet, Peter Freestone. Freddie's eyesight was failing. His spatial awareness and, therefore, his mobility was impaired. He would only ever use his antique furniture in Montreux a couple of times.

Freddie began to lose confidence in himself and started to avoid those he had partied with over the years. He didn't want his old friends to stand by, shake their heads and watch him deteriorate. On doctors' orders, he gave up drinking, smoking and other recreational habits. His doctors became his new friends; he could drop any act with them, he could ask them questions. Specialists were regular visitors to his home, a nurse would call to give him gruelling 12-hour blood transfusions which left him weaker still. But Freddie never complained. He and Joe Fanelli, who was also suffering from AIDS, read up all they could about possible treatments and medical developments. They never gave up hope. As long as he felt in control of the situation, Freddie would continue his projects in Montreux as best he could.

On 9 November 1991, Freddie flew back from Switzerland, having made up his mind; if the illness was taking hold of his life, he would take control back again. He told his partner, Jim, who was also suffering from AIDS, and his carers, Joe and Peter, that he would stop all medication except his painkillers. Freddie would decide when he would leave this world, if not the precise day. All business was conducted from his gigantic bed where his beloved cats lay within reach on the covers. Mary, now seven months' pregnant with her second child, visited him, so did his family, Brian and Roger from the band, Elton John, Dave Clark and others. On Friday 22 November 1991, Jim Beach, Queen's lawyer-manager and close friend in Montreux, came to the house. He had kept in touch with Freddie's doctors and understood the situation. He spent five-and-a-half hours with Freddie, discussing the singer's affairs in detail. It was decided to issue a statement to the press about his condition. Freddie had always held back from admitting he was ill, for fear of embarrassing his friends and family. Now he wanted his death to do some good, to make people aware that everyone was at risk. He felt it would do more good to make a public statement before he died; it would have more impact. But Freddie had no idea how little time he had left. Not much more than a day.

Freddie died peacefully in his bed at Garden Lodge, early on Sunday morning, 24 November 1991. The press, who had spent days outside his house, was kept behind police barricades while his body was removed from the house. His valet, Peter, organised the funeral; Freddie had asked to be cremated. Five hearses of flowers, three limousines and two private cars full of mourners, accompanied Freddie to West London Crematorium. The press was out in force and all the important people in

Freddie's life were there to say their goodbyes, including the three remaining members of Queen, Elton John and Dave Clark. Many others, like David Bowie, sent flowers from around the world. Bomi and Jer Bulsara had their son's ashes interred in the family Parsee plot near London. Mary would visit and lay flowers on the grave. Freddie's fans would make an annual pilgrimage to his home on the anniversary of his death where Mary would read out a message to them. Freddie had left her most of his wealth, his record royalties and his London home. His beautiful apartment in Montreux, the lease never having been finalised, reverted back to the bank and Mountain Studios was sold. A focal point for Freddie's fans was needed, somewhere they could celebrate his life and the pleasure his music had brought them. There was talk of a statue being erected in London, but the project never got off the ground.

Jim Beach, a permanent resident in Montreux, conferred with the Commune. On 25 November 1996, a magnificent three metres high bronze statue of Freddie, by the sculptor Irena Sedlecka, was installed on the waterfront, not far from where he recorded his last song, *Mother Love*, for the album *Made in Heaven* which was released in 1995. Singer of songs and lover of life, Freddie stands with his familiar half-microphone, legs astride, punching the air, looking out over his beloved Lake Geneva. The statue was unveiled by his father, Bomi Bulsara, and the opera singer, Montserrat Caballé. Fans continually festoon the statue with garlands of flowers, leave lighted candles and messages at his feet. Freddie, the eternal star, would have loved all that.

A tribute concert for Freddie was arranged by the rest of Queen and included contributions from Elton John, Liza Minelli, David Bowie, Annie Lennox, George Michael, Roger Daltrey and many others, and a speech by one of Freddie's favourite movie stars and near-neighbour in Switzerland, the tireless AIDS campaigner Elizabeth Taylor, who assured the audience she was not going to sing. The funds generated from the concert and other productions are redistributed by the Mercury Phoenix Trust, established in 1992 to help AIDS sufferers around the world. Now, fans gather in Montreux every first week in September for the 'Freddie Mercury Montreux Memorial Day'; his songs continue to break sales records and his fan club goes from strength to strength.

Not far from Freddie's statue, in front of the Montreux Palace hotel where Freddie first stayed when he came to Switzerland, sits writer Vladimir Nabokov's likeness, also cast in bronze, contemplating the same view. Further along the lakeside road, in Vevey, stands Charlie Chaplin, cast in bronze as the little man in his ill-fitting suit, bowler hat and with bent cane, gazing across the water to the same set of mountains, the Dents du Midi. The Swiss Riviera lost several members of its alpine set in 1991: Graham Greene passed away in Vevey in April, followed by Véra Nabokov, a few days later. Charlie Chaplin's wife, Oona, died at home in Corsier in September, followed, two months later, by Freddie Mercury in London.

Freddie always said that he composed *Killer Queen*, the stage-musical style song that shot him to stardom, with the singer-composer Noël Coward in mind. Just five minutes' journey from Montreux, in the picturesque alpine village of Les Avants, lived the multi-talented Noël Coward in a comfortable household situation not dissimilar to the one Freddie had established for himself in London. There were many similarities in the entertainers' lives: their talent to compose memorable tunes, their facility with words, their love of the good life, of male lovers, of Switzerland. Like Freddie, Noël worked hard and had his setbacks before he achieved wealth and fame. He moved in glittering circles, just as Freddie had glittered on stage in his harlequin leotard. The Glitterati who lived in Switzerland, stars such as Audrey Hepburn, Yul Brynner, Richard Burton, Elizabeth Taylor, Peter Ustinov, James Mason, David Niven, Peter Sellers and Noël Coward, knew each other well. Their lives were intertwined. But lives that glitter are not always golden, as we shall see in the next volume: *The Glitterati in Switzerland.*

Bibliography

The Man Who Wasn't Maigret: a Portrait of Georges Simenon Patrick Marnham Bloomsbury Publishing 1992

Simenon: a Biography Pierre Assouline Chatto and Windus 1997

Georges Simenon Lucille F Becker Haus Publishing 2006

My Autobiography Charles Chaplin Penguin Books 1992

Charlie Chaplin and His Times Kenneth S. Lynn Aurum Press 2002

Chaplin: His Life and Art David Robinson Penguin Books 2001

The Life of Graham Greene Volume One: 1904-1939 Norman Sherry Penguin Books 1989

The Life of Graham Greene Volume Two: 1939-1955 Norman Sherry Jonathan Cape 1994

The Life of Graham Greene Volume Three: 1955-1991 Norman Sherry Jonathan Cape 2004

Fragments of Autobiography: A Sort of Life and Ways of Escape Graham Greene Penguin Books 1991

Klop and the Ustinov family Nadia Benois Ustinov Sidgwick and Jackson 1973

Graham Greene: Friend and Brother Leopoldo Duran Fount Paperbacks 1995

A Preface to Greene Cedric Watts Longman Pearson Education Ltd 1997

Graham Greene: The Man Within Michael Shelden William Heinemann Ltd 1994

The Quest for Graham Greene W. J. West Weidenfeld & Nicholson 1997

The Third Woman William Cash Abacus 2001

In Search of a Beginning: My Life with Graham Greene Yvonne Cloetta Bloomsbury

A Dreadful Man Brian Aherne assisted by George Sanders and Benita Hume Simon and Schuster 1979

Memoirs of a Professional Cad George Sanders Hamish Hamilton 1960

George Sanders: An Exhausted Life Richard VanDerBeets Madison Books 1990

Before I Forget James Mason Hamish Hamilton 1981

James Mason: Odd Man Out Sheridan Morley
Weidenfeld and Nicholson 1989

James Mason's Ashes Are Finally Laid To Rest
Caroline Davies Telegraph Media Group Limited 2008

Portland Mason Telegraph Media Group Limited 2008

Illustrated Lives: Vladimir Nabokov Jane Grayson
Penguin Books 2001

VN: The Life and Art of Vladimir Nabokov Andrew
Field Futura Publications 1988

Vladimir Nabokov: The Russian Years Brian Boyd
Princeton University Press 1990

Vladimir Nabokov: The American Years Brian
Boyd Princeton University Press 1991

**Writers at Work The Paris Review Interviews
Fourth Series** Edited by George Plimpton Interview
with Herbert Gold Penguin Books 1985

Speak, Memory: An Autobiography Revisited
Vladimir Nabokov Penguin Classics 2000

Véra (Mrs Vladimir Nabokov) Stacy Schiff Modern
Library Paperbacks 2000

Lolita Vladimir Nabokov Penguin Red Classic 2006

Freddie Mercury: A Life, in His Own Words
Compiled and Edited by Greg Brooks and Simon Lupton
Mercury Songs Ltd 2006

Freddie Mercury: The Definitive Biography Lesley-Anne Jones Coronet Books 1997

Freddie Mercury: An Intimate Memoir By The Man Who Knew Him Best Peter Freestone with David Evans Omnibus Press 2001

XS All Areas: The Status Quo Autobiography
Francis Rossi and Rick Parfitt with Mick Wall Sidgwick & Jackson 2004

About the Author

Lindsay Greatwood was born in London, gained an Honours degree in English from the University of Sussex and taught English as a foreign language. She has ghost-written autobiographies for several personalities and published *Fame and Fortune in Switzerland: Audrey Hepburn, Richard Burton, Yul Brynner and other celebrity residents*. She lives in Switzerland with her Swiss francophone husband.

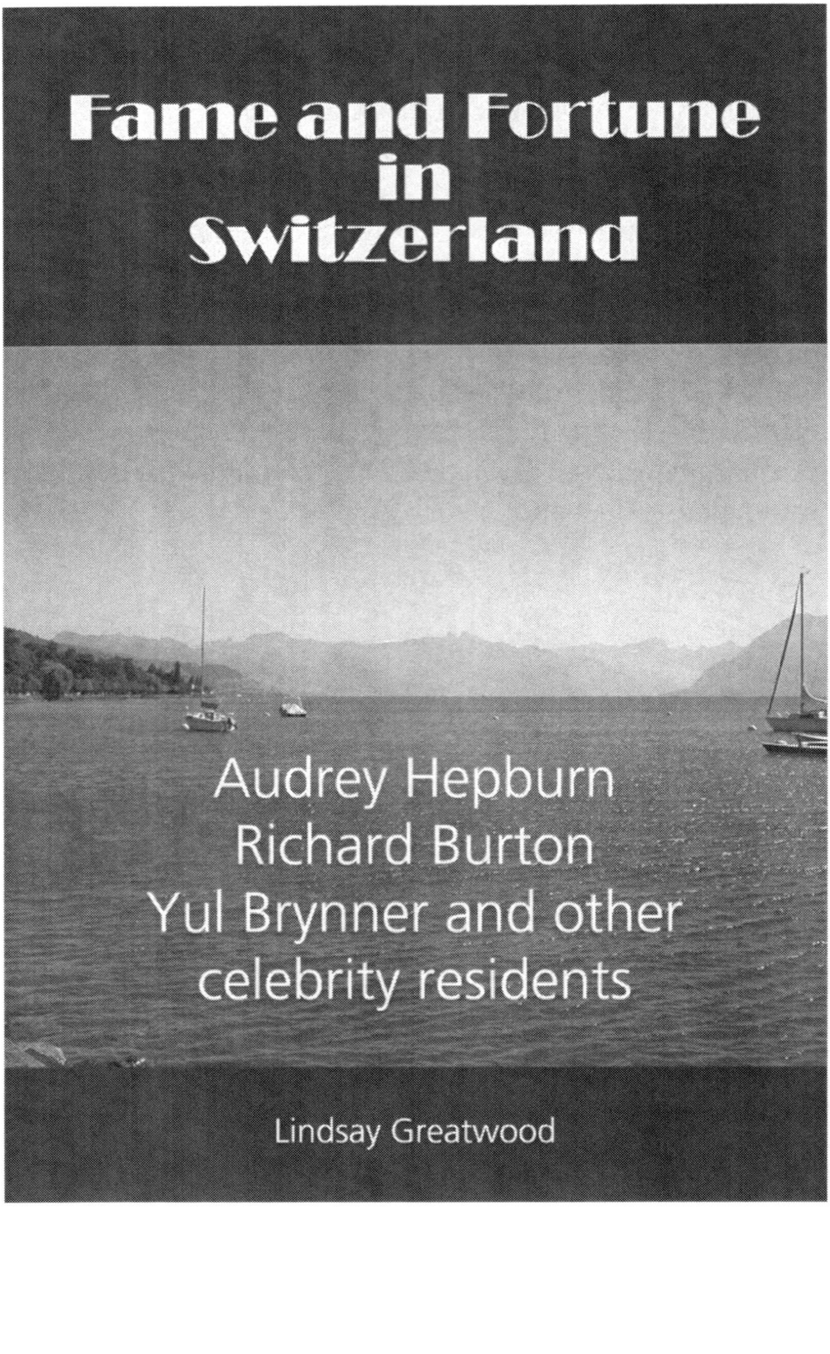
Fame and Fortune in Switzerland
Audrey Hepburn
Richard Burton
Yul Brynner and other
celebrity residents
Lindsay Greatwood

FAME AND FORTUNE
IN
SWITZERLAND

A number of well-known personalities were attracted to the shores of Lake Geneva in the second half of the twentieth century. Many of them knew each other well and their lives were intertwined. One or two fell deeply in love; others came to blows. Each faced more than one personal crisis, at least as dramatic as the situations they portrayed on screen or in print -

Ian Fleming: his time in Geneva coloured the world of James Bond

Richard Burton: the locals called his home a 'bicoque' – a shack

Alistair MacLean: a writer who came to blows with Burton

Peter Ustinov: took a long personal journey to a wine-growing region

Audrey Hepburn: fled from kidnappers to her 'place of peace'

Yul Brynner: lived in splendour on Lake Geneva

William Holden: fell in love with Audrey Hepburn

Coco Chanel: lived in exile after the war with her German lover

Capucine: jumped from the eighth floor of her apartment building

John James Publications
www.johnjamespublications.com

ISBN 978-2-8399-0509-1
9 782839 905091

Lightning Source UK Ltd.
Milton Keynes UK
22 August 2010

158761UK00001BA/93/P

9 782839 906609